Mastering
SUPER COMPUTING

Concepts, Techniques, and Applications

Nikhilesh Mishra,
Author

Website
https://www.nikhileshmishra.com

Copyright Information

Copyright © 2023 Nikhilesh Mishra

Dedication

This book is lovingly dedicated to the cherished memory of my father, **Late Krishna Gopal Mishra**, and my mother**, Mrs. Vijay Kanti Mishra.** Their unwavering support, guidance, and love continue to inspire me.

Table of Contents

Author's Preface

Welcome to the captivating world of the knowledge we are about to explore! Within these pages, we invite you to embark on a journey that delves into the frontiers of information and understanding.

Charting the Path to Knowledge

Dive deep into the subjects we are about to explore as we unravel the intricate threads of innovation, creativity, and problem-solving. Whether you're a curious enthusiast, a seasoned professional, or an eager learner, this book serves as your gateway to gaining a deeper understanding.

Your Guiding Light

From the foundational principles of our chosen field to the advanced frontiers of its applications, we've meticulously crafted this book to be your trusted companion. Each chapter is an expedition, guided by expertise and filled with practical insights to empower you on your quest for knowledge.

What Awaits You

- **Illuminate the Origins:** Embark on a journey through the historical evolution of our chosen field, discovering key milestones that have paved the way for breakthroughs.

- **Demystify Complex Concepts:** Grasp the fundamental principles, navigate intricate concepts, and explore practical applications.

- **Mastery of the Craft:** Equip yourself with the skills and knowledge needed to excel in our chosen domain.

Your Journey Begins Here

As we embark on this enlightening journey together, remember that mastery is not just about knowledge but also the wisdom to apply it. Let each chapter be a stepping stone towards unlocking your potential, and let this book be your guide to becoming a true connoisseur of our chosen field.

So, turn the page, delve into the chapters, and immerse yourself in the world of knowledge. Let curiosity be your compass, and let the pursuit of understanding be your guide.

Begin your expedition now. Your quest for mastery awaits!

Sincerely,

Nikhilesh Mishra,

Author

CHAPTER 1

Introduction to Supercomputing

In the vast landscape of modern technology, few fields command as much awe and admiration as supercomputing. Often heralded as the pinnacle of computational power, supercomputers are the giants of the digital age, capable of tackling some of humanity's most complex and pressing challenges. This chapter serves as our gateway into the world of supercomputing, where we embark on a journey to unravel the secrets behind these extraordinary machines.

Definition and Significance of Supercomputing

At its core, supercomputing represents the zenith of computing prowess. These machines are designed not merely to crunch numbers but to do so at an astonishing scale and speed. In this chapter, we will delve deep into the definition of supercomputing, exploring what sets it apart from conventional computing systems and why it holds such a pivotal role in various scientific, engineering, and research domains.

Mastering Supercomputing

Historical Evolution of Supercomputing

To understand the present and future of supercomputing, it's essential to trace its roots back in time. We'll embark on a historical journey, uncovering the pivotal milestones and developments that have shaped supercomputing into what it is today. From the early pioneers who laid the foundation to the race for exascale computing, this chapter offers a fascinating glimpse into the evolution of these remarkable machines.

Key Concepts: Parallel Processing, Scalability

Supercomputing isn't just about raw processing power; it's about harnessing that power efficiently. To achieve this, supercomputers employ advanced techniques such as parallel processing and scalability. We will demystify these key concepts, explaining how they enable supercomputers to tackle complex problems that would be insurmountable for conventional systems.

Benefits and Challenges of Supercomputing

While supercomputing offers unprecedented capabilities, it also comes with its own set of challenges. In this chapter, we will examine both the benefits and the hurdles that supercomputing brings to the table. From revolutionizing scientific discovery to the immense energy requirements, we'll explore the dual nature of these computational giants.

Setting Objectives for Learning About Supercomputing

Before we dive deeper into the intricacies of supercomputing, it's essential to set clear objectives for our journey. Whether you are a seasoned professional seeking to expand your knowledge or a newcomer intrigued by the possibilities, this chapter will help you define your goals and expectations as we navigate through the world of supercomputing.

Join us as we embark on this enlightening expedition into the heart of supercomputing, where computational boundaries are pushed to their limits, and the quest for knowledge knows no bounds.

A. Definition and Significance of Supercomputing

In the realm of information technology, supercomputing stands as a remarkable pinnacle, representing the zenith of computational capabilities. At its core, supercomputing can be defined as the utilization of highly advanced and exceptionally powerful computing systems specifically designed to perform complex and computationally intensive tasks. These tasks often involve intricate simulations, data analysis, modeling, and solving problems that demand an extraordinary amount of processing power and speed. Supercomputers achieve this by harnessing thousands, if not millions, of processing cores, working in concert to deliver unparalleled performance.

Significance of Supercomputing

The significance of supercomputing extends far beyond mere computational superiority; it transcends into several critical domains:

1. **Scientific Discovery and Research:** Supercomputers play an instrumental role in scientific endeavors across a wide spectrum of disciplines. From simulating the behavior of subatomic particles in particle physics to modeling the Earth's climate system, these machines enable scientists to conduct experiments and simulations that would otherwise be impossible. Supercomputing has led to groundbreaking discoveries in fields like astrophysics, chemistry, biology, and material science.

2. **Engineering and Design:** Engineers and designers employ supercomputers to simulate and analyze complex systems. Whether it's designing next-generation aircraft, optimizing the aerodynamics of automobiles, or modeling the behavior of structural materials, supercomputers are indispensable for ensuring safety, efficiency, and innovation in engineering.

3. **Medical Research and Drug Discovery:** The healthcare sector benefits immensely from supercomputing's computational prowess. Researchers use supercomputers for

tasks like protein folding simulations, drug interactions modeling, and genomic analysis. These applications hold the potential to revolutionize medicine by accelerating drug discovery and personalizing treatment approaches.

4. **Weather and Climate Prediction:** Supercomputers are the backbone of weather forecasting and climate modeling. They process vast amounts of data from satellites, weather stations, and sensors to create highly detailed and accurate weather forecasts. In the realm of climate science, supercomputers are vital for understanding long-term climate trends and predicting the impact of climate change.

5. **National Security:** Governments worldwide rely on supercomputers for national security and defense applications. These machines are used for cryptography, nuclear weapons simulations, and intelligence analysis. They play a critical role in ensuring the security of nations.

6. **Space Exploration:** In the quest to explore our universe, supercomputing is indispensable. It aids in trajectory calculations, space mission simulations, and the analysis of data from space telescopes and probes. Supercomputers have contributed significantly to our understanding of the cosmos.

7. **Economic Competitiveness:** Supercomputing is a strategic asset for countries and industries aiming to maintain a competitive edge. It drives innovation, product development,

and economic growth by enabling organizations to solve complex problems more efficiently.

8. **Challenges and Problem-Solving:** Beyond specific domains, supercomputers are used to address global challenges. They tackle problems like predicting natural disasters, optimizing transportation networks, and managing energy resources, making them invaluable tools for addressing complex societal issues.

In summary, supercomputing is not merely a technological achievement; it is a catalyst for scientific progress, innovation, and addressing some of the world's most pressing challenges. Its significance extends to virtually every aspect of modern life, making it a field of paramount importance in the world of computing and technology.

B. Historical Evolution of Supercomputing

The history of supercomputing is a captivating journey that reflects the relentless human pursuit of computational power and the relentless drive to solve increasingly complex problems. The evolution of supercomputing can be traced through several key milestones:

1. Emergence of the Precursors (1940s-1950s): The roots of supercomputing can be found in the early electronic computers of the 1940s and 1950s. Pioneering machines like the ENIAC (Electronic Numerical Integrator and Computer) and UNIVAC (Universal Automatic Computer) marked the beginning of electronic computing. While these early computers were large and slow by today's standards, they laid the foundation for what was to come.

2. Seymour Cray and CDC (1960s-1970s): The true birth of supercomputing as we know it can be attributed to Seymour Cray, an engineer who founded Cray Research, Inc. In the 1960s and 1970s, Cray and his team developed a series of groundbreaking supercomputers, including the CDC 6600 and the Cray-1. These machines introduced vector processing, a technique that allowed a single instruction to operate on multiple pieces of data simultaneously, significantly boosting computational speed.

3. Rise of Parallel Processing (1980s): The 1980s marked a significant shift in supercomputing with the introduction of parallel processing. Instead of relying solely on single, extremely fast processors, supercomputers began to incorporate multiple processors working in parallel. This approach dramatically increased computational power. Notable supercomputers from this era include the Cray X-MP and the Connection Machine.

4. Beowulf Clusters and Massively Parallel Processing (1990s): The 1990s saw the rise of Beowulf clusters, a cost-effective way to build supercomputers using off-the-shelf components and open-source software. This democratization of supercomputing allowed research institutions and universities to harness considerable computing power. Concurrently, machines like the Cray T3E and IBM's Blue Gene series pushed the boundaries of massively parallel processing.

5. Entry into the Terabyte Era (2000s): Supercomputing entered the terascale era in the early 2000s, with machines like IBM's ASCI White becoming the first supercomputer to achieve sustained teraflop (trillion floating-point operations per second) performance. The TOP500 list, which ranks the world's fastest supercomputers, became a barometer of this rapid progress.

6. Path to Exascale (2010s-2020s): As computational demands continued to surge, supercomputing entered the exascale era, aiming to reach one exaflop (a quintillion calculations per second). The development of exascale supercomputers involves overcoming immense technical challenges, particularly in power consumption and heat management. Countries like China, the United States, and Japan are competing in this race to build the first exascale machines.

7. Diverse Architectures and Quantum Computing (Current and Future): Today's supercomputing landscape features a diverse array of architectures, including traditional CPU-based systems, GPU-accelerated machines, and even emerging quantum supercomputers. Quantum computing, in particular, represents a paradigm shift in computing, promising to solve problems that are currently beyond the reach of classical supercomputers.

The historical evolution of supercomputing is a testament to human ingenuity and our unyielding quest to push the boundaries of what is computationally possible. It's a journey that continues to unfold, promising even more astonishing advancements in the years to come, and with the emergence of quantum computing, the future of supercomputing holds boundless possibilities.

C. Key Concepts: Parallel Processing and Scalability

Supercomputing's exceptional computational power doesn't solely rely on raw clock speed or the number of processors. Instead, it hinges on two fundamental concepts: parallel processing and scalability. These concepts are the bedrock upon which supercomputers achieve unparalleled performance and handle complex tasks efficiently.

Parallel Processing: The Power of Simultaneity

Parallel processing refers to the simultaneous execution of multiple tasks, instructions, or processes, all orchestrated to work in concert toward a common goal. In essence, it's the ability to divide a computational problem into smaller, manageable subproblems and tackle them concurrently, significantly accelerating the overall computation. Parallel processing is the key to harnessing the full potential of modern supercomputers. It can be broken down into several important aspects:

1. **Data Parallelism:** In data parallelism, a single task is divided into smaller sub-tasks, and each sub-task operates on a different set of data. This approach is common in tasks like matrix operations, image processing, and simulations where the same operation needs to be performed on a large dataset.

2. **Task Parallelism:** Task parallelism involves dividing a task into smaller, independent tasks that can be executed concurrently. This is often used in applications where different components of a complex computation can be performed in parallel without requiring much communication between them.

3. **Hybrid Parallelism:** Many modern supercomputers employ a hybrid approach, combining both data and task parallelism. This allows for maximum utilization of available resources and is well-suited for diverse workloads.

Scalability: The Art of Growing Efficiently

While parallel processing enables supercomputers to tackle complex problems, *scalability* determines how well a system can adapt as its computational requirements grow. Scalability isn't just about adding more processors; it's about doing so in a way that maintains or even improves performance without introducing bottlenecks or excessive overhead. Several key aspects of scalability include:

1. **Horizontal Scalability:** Also known as "scaling out," this involves adding more computational nodes or processing units to a supercomputer. This approach aims to distribute the workload across multiple machines and is typically achieved through technologies like clusters and grids.

2. **Vertical Scalability:** In contrast to horizontal scalability, "vertical scalability" or "scaling up" involves adding more resources to a single machine, such as increasing the number of processors, memory, or storage capacity. This approach is often used in shared-memory supercomputers.

3. **Load Balancing:** To ensure optimal performance, supercomputers must distribute work evenly among available processing units. Load balancing algorithms are essential to achieve this, preventing some processors from becoming idle while others are overwhelmed.

4. **Fault Tolerance:** As the number of components in a supercomputer increases, so does the likelihood of hardware failures. Scalable systems incorporate fault-tolerant mechanisms to detect and recover from failures without disrupting ongoing computations.

5. **Scalability Metrics:** Performance metrics like "strong scaling" and "weak scaling" help evaluate how efficiently a supercomputer scales as the problem size or computational resources increase. Strong scaling measures performance for a fixed problem size, while weak scaling evaluates performance as the problem size grows proportionally with resources.

In the world of supercomputing, the synergy of parallel processing and scalability allows machines to take on challenges that were once considered insurmountable. These concepts empower supercomputers to excel in a wide array of applications, from simulating complex physical phenomena to solving intricate mathematical problems, all while pushing the boundaries of what's computationally achievable. As supercomputing continues to evolve, parallelism and scalability remain essential principles guiding its advancement.

D. Benefits of Supercomputing

Supercomputing is a powerful and transformative technology that offers a wide range of benefits across various domains. These benefits have a profound impact on scientific research, industry, and society as a whole:

1. **Scientific Advancement:** Supercomputers enable scientists to simulate complex natural phenomena, from the behavior of subatomic particles to the dynamics of the universe. They

facilitate scientific discovery by accelerating simulations and enabling researchers to explore scenarios that would be impractical or impossible with conventional computing resources.

2. **Medical Breakthroughs:** In the field of healthcare, supercomputers play a critical role in drug discovery, genomics, and personalized medicine. They can analyze massive datasets, simulate drug interactions, and model complex biological processes, leading to the development of new treatments and therapies.

3. **Engineering and Design:** Supercomputing is indispensable for industries such as aerospace, automotive, and architecture. Engineers use supercomputers to perform complex simulations, optimize designs, and test prototypes in virtual environments. This reduces development time and costs while improving product performance and safety.

4. **Weather and Climate Prediction:** Supercomputers drive advances in meteorology and climate science. They process vast amounts of data from satellites, weather stations, and sensors to create highly accurate weather forecasts. In climate science, supercomputers help model climate change and assess its impact on the planet.

5. **National Security:** Governments utilize supercomputers for defense applications, including cryptography, nuclear

weapons simulations, and intelligence analysis. These machines are essential for ensuring national security and addressing emerging threats.

6. **Energy and Environment:** Supercomputers contribute to energy efficiency and sustainability efforts by simulating energy systems, optimizing power grids, and modeling renewable energy sources. They also aid in environmental research by simulating ecosystem dynamics and assessing the impact of pollution.

7. **Economic Competitiveness:** Supercomputing enhances a country's economic competitiveness by driving innovation, supporting advanced manufacturing, and promoting research and development. Nations with strong supercomputing capabilities have a competitive edge in global markets.

Challenges of Supercomputing

While supercomputing offers remarkable benefits, it also presents several significant challenges:

1. **Cost:** Building and maintaining supercomputers is expensive. The initial hardware and infrastructure costs, along with ongoing operational expenses, can strain budgets. This is especially challenging for academic and research institutions with limited resources.

2. **Power Consumption:** Supercomputers are power-hungry machines that consume vast amounts of electricity. Addressing their energy demands is crucial for sustainability and cost management. Many supercomputing centers are investing in energy-efficient technologies.

3. **Programming Complexity:** Harnessing the full potential of supercomputers often requires specialized programming skills. Parallel programming, in particular, can be complex and error-prone. Developing software that efficiently utilizes the available resources remains a challenge.

4. **Heat Dissipation:** The intense computational activity generates significant heat, requiring sophisticated cooling systems to prevent overheating. Heat dissipation is a critical aspect of supercomputer design and operation.

5. **Data Management:** Supercomputers generate enormous volumes of data. Storing, managing, and transferring this data efficiently pose challenges. Researchers must develop strategies for data handling, including storage and backup solutions.

6. **Security Concerns:** Supercomputers are attractive targets for cyberattacks due to their computational power and access to sensitive data. Ensuring robust cybersecurity measures is essential to protect these machines and the valuable information they process.

7. **Scalability:** As computational demands continue to grow, scaling supercomputers to meet these demands while maintaining efficiency can be challenging. Achieving scalability without introducing bottlenecks or performance degradation is an ongoing concern.

8. **Maintenance and Upgrades:** Supercomputers require regular maintenance and upgrades to remain competitive. Keeping up with advancements in hardware and software technology is essential to ensure their continued relevance.

In conclusion, supercomputing offers immense benefits in terms of scientific discovery, innovation, and problem-solving capabilities across various fields. However, addressing the associated challenges, including cost, power consumption, programming complexity, and security, is essential to maximize the potential of supercomputing while mitigating its drawbacks. As technology continues to advance, supercomputing will play an increasingly vital role in addressing complex and pressing global challenges.

E. Setting Objectives for Learning About Supercomputing

Learning about supercomputing is a journey into the world of unparalleled computational power and its applications in various domains. Whether you are a seasoned professional seeking to deepen your knowledge or a newcomer intrigued by the possibilities of supercomputing, setting clear objectives is a crucial first step in maximizing the value of your learning experience. Here's why it matters and how to go about it:

1. Define Your Learning Goals:

- **Expertise Level:** Begin by assessing your current knowledge and experience in computing. Are you a beginner looking for an introduction to supercomputing, or do you have some background and want to delve deeper into advanced topics?

- **Application Focus:** Consider your specific interests and how supercomputing can benefit your field. Are you interested in scientific research, engineering, healthcare, finance, or another domain where supercomputers are used?

- **Skill Development:** Determine which skills you want to acquire or enhance. Supercomputing involves various aspects, including programming, parallel computing, data analysis, and system administration. Identifying your skill development goals will guide your learning path.

2. Understand the Scope of Supercomputing:

- **Supercomputer Types:** Gain a basic understanding of the different types of supercomputers, such as cluster supercomputers, vector supercomputers, massively parallel processing (MPP) systems, and emerging technologies like quantum supercomputers. Knowing the landscape will help you choose a suitable focus.

- **Applications:** Explore the diverse applications of supercomputing across fields like scientific research, healthcare, engineering, and finance. Identify specific use cases that align with your interests and objectives.

3. Tailor Your Learning Path:

- **Select Learning Resources:** Identify reliable learning resources that match your objectives. These can include textbooks, online courses, tutorials, academic institutions, and supercomputing centers that offer training programs.

- **Programming Languages:** Depending on your goals, decide which programming languages are relevant to your learning objectives. For example, Python, C/C++, and languages like CUDA for GPU programming may be essential.

- **Hands-On Practice:** Incorporate hands-on practice into your learning plan. Experimenting with supercomputing tools, libraries, and programming environments will solidify your understanding and skills.

4. Seek Guidance and Mentorship:

- **Connect with Experts:** Reach out to experts in the field of supercomputing through forums, conferences, and professional networks. Learning from experienced practitioners can provide valuable insights and guidance.

- **Mentorship:** Consider finding a mentor who can provide one-on-one guidance and support as you navigate your learning journey. A mentor can offer personalized advice and help you stay on track.

5. Measure Progress and Adjust:

- **Assessment:** Regularly assess your progress towards your learning objectives. Set milestones to track your development and identify areas that may require additional attention.

- **Flexibility:** Be flexible in adjusting your objectives as you learn. As your understanding of supercomputing deepens, you may discover new areas of interest or refine your goals.

6. Stay Informed and Engage with the Community:

- **Stay Updated:** Supercomputing is a rapidly evolving field. Stay informed about the latest advancements, technologies, and best practices by following industry news, attending conferences, and reading research papers.

- **Community Engagement:** Engage with the supercomputing community through online forums, social media, and professional organizations. Participating in discussions and networking can provide valuable insights and opportunities for collaboration.

Setting clear objectives for learning about supercomputing is essential to ensure a structured and fulfilling learning experience. Whether your goal is to become a supercomputing expert, apply supercomputing techniques to your work, or simply gain a broad understanding of this transformative technology, a well-defined learning path will help you make the most of your journey. Supercomputing has the potential to open doors to groundbreaking research and innovation, and your objectives will guide you toward realizing that potential.

CHAPTER 2

Parallel Computing Fundamentals

In the ever-expanding landscape of computing, the concept of parallelism stands as a cornerstone of modern computational prowess. Parallel computing is not merely a technical innovation; it is a paradigm shift that has redefined the limits of what we can achieve with computational resources. This chapter serves as your gateway into the captivating realm of parallel computing, where we will unravel the fundamental principles that underpin the extraordinary power of parallelism.

Parallel Processing and Its Importance

At its essence, parallel computing revolves around the concept of simultaneous execution. It's the art of breaking down complex problems into smaller, manageable tasks and executing them concurrently, harnessing the collective might of multiple processing units. This chapter delves deep into the concept of parallel processing, explaining why it's a game-changer in the world of computing. We will explore how parallelism boosts computational speed, enabling us to tackle problems that were once considered insurmountable.

Types of Parallelism: Data, Task, Hybrid

Parallelism comes in various forms, each tailored to specific computational challenges. In this chapter, we will dissect the three primary types of parallelism: data parallelism, task parallelism, and the hybrid approach that combines both. You'll gain insights into when and how to apply these forms of parallelism effectively, ensuring that you have the right tools for the job.

Parallel Architectures: SIMD, MIMD

Supercomputers owe much of their extraordinary performance to specialized architectures designed for parallel processing. We will explore two fundamental parallel architectures: Single Instruction, Multiple Data (SIMD), and Multiple Instruction, Multiple Data (MIMD). Understanding these architectures is vital to harnessing the full potential of parallel computing.

Message Passing and Shared Memory Models

To achieve efficient parallelism, supercomputers rely on distinct programming models, namely the message passing and shared memory models. This chapter will unravel the intricacies of these models, clarifying how they enable communication and synchronization among parallel processes.

Scalability and Performance Metrics

Parallel computing's true test lies in its scalability—how

effectively it can adapt to increased computational demands. We will explore the critical concept of scalability and the performance metrics used to measure the efficiency of parallel systems. Understanding these principles is essential for building and optimizing supercomputers that can tackle challenges of ever-growing complexity.

Join us as we embark on this illuminating exploration of parallel computing fundamentals. Whether you are a seasoned computational scientist, a programmer looking to harness the power of parallelism, or a curious newcomer to the world of high-performance computing, this chapter will equip you with the knowledge and tools to unlock the full potential of parallel processing. Parallel computing is not just a technological advancement; it is a paradigm that reshapes the boundaries of what is computationally achievable, and in this chapter, we begin the journey of understanding its profound significance.

A. Parallel Processing and Its Importance

Parallel processing is a foundational concept in the field of computing, revolutionizing the way complex computational tasks are handled. At its core, parallel processing refers to the simultaneous execution of multiple tasks or processes, orchestrated to work in harmony toward a common objective. This paradigm shift has transformed computing, offering a myriad of benefits that are vital in the modern era:

1. Speed and Performance Enhancement:

- *Simultaneous Execution:* In traditional sequential processing, a computer executes instructions one after the other. In contrast, parallel processing allows multiple instructions or tasks to be carried out simultaneously, significantly increasing computational speed.

- *Tackling Large Datasets:* Parallel processing is especially valuable for handling massive datasets and performing complex calculations. Tasks that would take an impractical amount of time with sequential processing can be completed swiftly.

2. Scalability:

- *Adapting to Growing Demands:* As computational demands increase, parallel systems can scale efficiently by adding more processing units. This scalability ensures that computing resources can meet the needs of ever-expanding datasets and complex problems.

- *Resource Optimization:* Parallelism allows for the efficient utilization of available hardware resources. Rather than relying on a single, extremely fast processor, it harnesses the power of multiple processors or cores, distributing the workload and preventing resource bottlenecks.

3. Problem Solving:

- *Complex Problem Solving:* Parallel processing is instrumental in tackling complex problems that require immense computational power. It is used extensively in scientific simulations, weather forecasting, cryptography, and advanced mathematical modeling.

- *Real-time Applications:* In real-time applications like video editing, gaming, and financial trading, parallel processing ensures that tasks are executed swiftly without noticeable delays, enhancing user experiences.

4. Improved Resource Utilization:

- *Energy Efficiency:* Parallel processing can lead to energy efficiency gains because it allows tasks to be distributed across multiple processors, reducing the need for a single, power-hungry processor to handle all the workload.

- *Resource Allocation:* In data centers and cloud computing environments, parallel processing enables efficient resource allocation. Virtual machines and containers can be run in parallel on a single server, maximizing resource utilization.

5. Scientific and Engineering Advances:

- *Scientific Discovery:* Parallel processing has played a pivotal role in scientific breakthroughs by enabling simulations of natural phenomena, such as climate modeling, particle physics, and astrophysics. Researchers can explore scenarios that were previously computationally infeasible.

- *Engineering and Design:* Industries like aerospace, automotive, and architecture rely on parallel processing for simulations and optimizations. Engineers can design and test prototypes virtually, reducing development time and costs.

6. Parallel Programming and Paradigms:

- *Parallel Programming Models:* To harness the power of parallel processing, programmers use parallel programming models like MPI (Message Passing Interface) and OpenMP. These models provide the tools and frameworks for developing parallel applications.

- *Hybrid Computing:* Many modern supercomputers and high-performance computing clusters employ a hybrid approach, combining both parallel processing and distributed computing techniques to maximize performance and efficiency.

In summary, parallel processing has revolutionized computing by offering substantial speed and performance improvements, scalability, and the capability to address complex problems across various domains. It has become an essential component of modern computing systems, enabling advancements in science, engineering, and technology. As computational demands continue to grow, parallel processing remains indispensable in pushing the boundaries of what is computationally achievable.

B. Types of Parallelism: Data, Task, Hybrid

Parallel computing derives its power from dividing a complex problem into smaller, more manageable tasks and executing them concurrently. The three primary types of parallelism—Data, Task, and Hybrid—each offer unique approaches to achieving parallel processing efficiency, depending on the nature of the problem and the available computing resources.

1. Data Parallelism:

Definition: Data parallelism is a parallel computing paradigm where the same operation is applied simultaneously to multiple pieces of data. Essentially, it involves dividing a data set into smaller segments and performing identical operations on each segment concurrently.

Key Characteristics:

- **Simultaneous Data Processing:** In data parallelism, multiple processing units, such as CPU cores or GPU threads, work in parallel to process different portions of the same dataset.

- **Embarrassingly Parallel Problems:** Data parallelism is particularly well-suited for problems that can be divided into completely independent subproblems. These are often referred to as "embarrassingly parallel" problems.

- **High Throughput:** Data parallelism excels at achieving high throughput, making it ideal for applications like image and video processing, scientific simulations involving grid-based calculations, and many forms of data analysis.

Example: Image Processing

- In image processing, data parallelism can be used to apply the same filter or transformation to different regions of an image simultaneously. For example, when applying a blur filter to an image, each pixel's value can be updated independently, allowing for faster image processing.

2. Task Parallelism:

Definition: Task parallelism is a parallel computing paradigm where different tasks or sub-tasks are executed concurrently. In this approach, tasks may perform different operations, and coordination is required among them to achieve a common goal.

Key Characteristics:

- **Independent Task Execution:** Task parallelism is employed when tasks are largely independent but must cooperate or share data to complete a larger computation. Tasks can have different functionalities.

- **Workflow Coordination:** A key aspect of task parallelism is managing the coordination and communication between tasks. This often involves synchronization mechanisms to ensure proper task sequencing.

- **Flexibility:** Task parallelism is versatile and well-suited for applications where tasks may have varying computational requirements or where certain tasks may be optional or conditional.

Example: Video Editing

- In video editing software, task parallelism is used to perform different operations on a video, such as video decoding, audio processing, and graphical effects rendering, concurrently. These tasks are largely independent but need to be coordinated to produce the final edited video.

3. Hybrid Parallelism:

Definition: Hybrid parallelism is a combination of both data parallelism and task parallelism. It leverages the strengths of both approaches to achieve efficient parallel processing, making it suitable for complex applications.

Key Characteristics:

- **Mixing Parallelism Types:** Hybrid parallelism allows for the use of data parallelism within tasks or subcomponents that benefit from it, while also employing task parallelism for coordinating the execution of these tasks.

- **Balancing Workloads:** It enables a finer-grained control of parallelism, allowing for workload balancing, where certain tasks can be parallelized with data parallelism, and others can be executed in a more task-oriented manner.

- **Optimal Resource Utilization:** Hybrid parallelism is often employed in high-performance computing environments and supercomputers to optimize resource utilization and achieve maximum performance.

Example: Molecular Dynamics Simulation

- In a molecular dynamics simulation, hybrid parallelism can be used. Data parallelism may be employed to compute forces between atoms within a molecule, while task parallelism can coordinate the simulation of different molecules or sections of a larger molecular system.

In practice, choosing the right type of parallelism depends on the specific characteristics of the problem at hand, the available hardware resources, and the desired performance goals. Hybrid parallelism, combining data and task parallelism, is often favored for complex applications that require both fine-grained data manipulation and task-level coordination to achieve optimal parallel processing efficiency. Understanding these parallelism types is essential for designing efficient parallel algorithms and utilizing the full potential of parallel computing systems.

C. Parallel Architectures: SIMD and MIMD

Parallel architectures are the fundamental building blocks of supercomputers and high-performance computing systems. They dictate how processing units execute instructions and manage data to achieve parallelism. The two most common parallel architectures are SIMD and MIMD, each with its own set of characteristics and applications.

1. SIMD (Single Instruction, Multiple Data):

Definition: SIMD, which stands for Single Instruction, Multiple Data, is a parallel computing architecture in which a single instruction is executed by multiple processing elements simultaneously, but each processing element operates on a different piece of data. It's like having a group of workers all performing the same task independently but on different data elements.

Key Characteristics:

- **Single Instruction Stream:** In SIMD architecture, a single instruction stream is dispatched to all processing elements. This means that every processing element performs the same operation at the same time.

- **Data Parallelism:** SIMD excels in data parallelism, where the same operation needs to be applied to a large dataset. It's highly efficient for tasks like matrix operations, image processing, and vector calculations.

- **Synchronization:** SIMD processing elements operate synchronously, which means that they are tightly synchronized in their execution. This synchronization can be beneficial for certain applications but also imposes limitations on the flexibility of the architecture.

Applications:

- SIMD architectures are commonly used in applications where the same operation needs to be applied to a large dataset simultaneously. Examples include graphics processing units (GPUs), which accelerate tasks like rendering and scientific simulations involving large datasets.

- SIMD instructions are also found in modern CPUs and are used for tasks like multimedia processing, encryption, and 3D graphics rendering.

2. MIMD (Multiple Instruction, Multiple Data):

Definition: MIMD, or Multiple Instruction, Multiple Data, is a parallel computing architecture in which multiple processing elements execute different instructions on separate sets of data independently. It's like having multiple workers, each performing a unique task on their own set of data.

Key Characteristics:

- **Multiple Instruction Streams:** MIMD architectures allow for multiple instruction streams, meaning that each processing element can execute its own set of instructions independently of others.

- **Task Parallelism:** MIMD is highly suited for task parallelism, where different tasks or processes need to be executed concurrently. Each processing element can work on distinct tasks, making it versatile for a wide range of applications.

- **Asynchronous Execution:** In MIMD, processing elements operate asynchronously, meaning they are not necessarily synchronized in their execution. This flexibility allows for diverse and independently progressing tasks.

Applications:

- MIMD architectures are found in a wide range of computing systems, including multi-core CPUs, clusters of computers, and supercomputers. They are versatile and can be used for various parallel applications.

- MIMD systems are well-suited for scientific simulations, parallel algorithms, and applications that involve diverse tasks, such as weather forecasting, finite element analysis, and distributed computing.

Hybrid Architectures:

In some cases, supercomputers and high-performance computing clusters employ hybrid architectures that combine elements of both SIMD and MIMD to maximize performance and efficiency. These systems often leverage the strengths of SIMD for data parallelism and MIMD for task parallelism within a single machine.

Understanding the characteristics and capabilities of both SIMD and MIMD architectures is crucial for designing efficient parallel algorithms and choosing the right hardware for specific computational tasks. Different applications may benefit more from one architecture than the other, or even from a combination of both in a hybrid system, depending on their parallelism requirements and computational demands.

D. Message Passing and Shared Memory Models

Message Passing and Shared Memory Models are two fundamental programming paradigms used in parallel computing to facilitate communication and coordination among parallel processes or threads. These models are essential for ensuring that parallel tasks work together effectively to solve complex problems. Here's an in-depth look at each model:

1. Message Passing Model:

Definition: In the Message Passing Model, parallel processes or threads communicate by sending and receiving messages. Each process has its own memory space and operates independently. Communication occurs explicitly through message passing, where data is copied from one process's memory to another.

Key Characteristics:

- **Distributed Memory:** In this model, each process has its own distinct memory space. Processes do not share memory, making it suitable for distributed computing environments, clusters, and supercomputers.

- **Explicit Communication:** Processes must explicitly send and receive messages to share data or synchronize their execution. This communication is typically managed through communication libraries like MPI (Message Passing Interface) or PVM (Parallel Virtual Machine).

- **Scalability:** The Message Passing Model is highly scalable, as it allows processes to communicate across multiple nodes or processors. This scalability is crucial for tackling large-scale parallel problems.

- **Complex Coordination:** While message passing provides fine-grained control over communication, it can result in complex coordination when dealing with large numbers of processes or intricate communication patterns.

Applications:

- Scientific simulations, where different processes represent parts of a physical domain (e.g., particles in a molecular dynamics simulation).

- Distributed computing applications that run on clusters or grids, such as distributed data processing or web services.

- Many high-performance computing (HPC) applications in areas like weather modeling, computational chemistry, and astrophysics rely on the Message Passing Model for efficient parallelization.

2. Shared Memory Model:

Definition: In the Shared Memory Model, parallel processes or threads share a common address space or memory region. Each process can read from and write to this shared memory, which simplifies communication and data sharing.

Key Characteristics:

- **Shared Memory Space:** All processes in the system have access to the same global memory space. This shared memory is often organized as a shared data structure or an array.

- **Implicit Communication:** Unlike the Message Passing Model, processes in the Shared Memory Model do not need to explicitly send and receive messages to communicate. They share data directly through memory reads and writes.

- **Synchronization:** As processes can access shared data simultaneously, synchronization mechanisms such as locks, semaphores, and barriers are essential to prevent data conflicts and ensure coordinated execution.

- **Limited Scalability:** The Shared Memory Model is limited in scalability because the shared memory becomes a bottleneck as the number of processes increases. It is more suitable for multi-core processors or small-scale parallelism.

Applications:

- Multi-threaded applications running on multi-core processors, where threads share data and coordinate their activities through shared memory.

- Symmetric multiprocessing (SMP) systems that utilize multiple processors or cores within a single machine, as they provide a shared memory architecture.

- Some parallel algorithms, such as parallel sorting or graph algorithms, are naturally suited for the Shared Memory Model due to their need for shared data structures.

Hybrid Models:

In many real-world scenarios, hybrid models that combine elements of both message passing and shared memory are used to optimize performance. These models leverage the strengths of each approach to strike a balance between fine-grained control (message passing) and ease of communication (shared memory) while adapting to the specific characteristics of the application and hardware architecture.

In summary, the choice between Message Passing and Shared Memory Models depends on the nature of the parallel problem, the hardware architecture, and the desired level of control and coordination. Message passing is well-suited for distributed systems and complex communication patterns, while shared memory simplifies communication but may be limited in scalability. Hybrid models offer flexibility to address a broader range of parallel computing challenges. Understanding these models is essential for effective parallel programming and leveraging the full potential of parallel computing resources.

E. Scalability and Performance Metrics

Scalability and performance metrics are crucial aspects of parallel computing, helping to assess and optimize the efficiency of parallel applications. These concepts are particularly vital as the size and complexity of computational problems continue to grow. Here's an in-depth look at scalability and various performance metrics:

Scalability:

Definition: Scalability refers to the ability of a parallel computing system or application to handle increasing workloads efficiently as more resources are added. In essence, it measures how well a system can grow to accommodate larger problems or take advantage of additional hardware resources.

Key Characteristics:

- **Workload Growth:** Scalability evaluates how the performance of a parallel system or application evolves as the size of the problem or the number of parallel processes increases. Ideally, performance should improve or remain consistent with increased resources.

- **Linear Scaling:** Perfect scalability would mean that doubling the resources (e.g., processors or cores) would halve the execution time, resulting in a linear speedup. Achieving linear scalability is rare in practice due to factors like communication overhead and synchronization.

- **Types of Scalability:** There are two main types of scalability:

  1. **Strong Scalability:** Measures how well an application can handle a fixed-size problem as the number of processors or cores increases. The goal is to reduce the time to solution as resources grow.

  2. **Weak Scalability:** Assesses how efficiently an application can solve larger problems as the number of processors or cores increases proportionally with the problem size. The objective is to maintain a constant workload per processor.

- **Amdahl's Law:** Amdahl's Law is a theoretical model that illustrates the limits of speedup in parallel computing. It emphasizes the importance of optimizing the serial (non-parallel) portion of an application, as it can significantly impact overall performance.

Importance of Scalability:

- **Resource Utilization:** Scalability ensures that resources, such as processors, memory, and storage, are used effectively to solve increasingly complex problems without wasted computational power.

- **Cost Efficiency:** For large-scale parallel systems, scalability is critical for cost efficiency. It enables organizations to meet computational demands without adding unnecessary hardware and operational costs.

- **Time to Solution:** Scalability directly impacts the time it takes to solve complex problems. Efficiently scaling an application can lead to faster results, which is crucial in fields like scientific research and engineering.

Performance Metrics:

Performance metrics are used to evaluate the efficiency and effectiveness of parallel applications. They provide quantifiable measures of how well an application is utilizing available resources and achieving its objectives. Some common performance metrics include:

1. **Speedup (S):** Speedup measures how much faster a parallel application runs compared to its sequential counterpart. It is calculated as $S = T(1) / T(p)$, where $T(1)$ is the execution time on a single processor, and $T(p)$ is the execution time on p processors. Higher speedup values indicate better parallel performance.

2. **Efficiency (E):** Efficiency quantifies how efficiently a parallel application uses additional processors or cores. It is calculated as E = Speedup / p, where p is the number of processors. Efficiency values range from 0 to 1, with 1 indicating perfect efficiency.

3. **Scalability (Sc):** Scalability measures the ability of an application to effectively use additional resources. It is calculated as $Sc = T(1) / (p * T(p))$, where $T(1)$ is the execution time on a single processor, $T(p)$ is the execution time on p processors. Scalability values greater than 1 suggest good scalability.

4. **Load Balance:** Load balance assesses how evenly the computational workload is distributed among parallel processes or threads. An ideal load balance ensures that all processes finish their tasks simultaneously, minimizing idle time.

5. **Communication Overhead:** Communication overhead measures the time and resources consumed by processes in a parallel application for exchanging data and synchronization. High communication overhead can hinder scalability.

6. **Memory Usage:** Memory metrics evaluate the memory requirements of a parallel application. This includes assessing memory consumption, data transfer rates, and memory bandwidth.

7. **Flop/s (Floating-Point Operations Per Second):** Flop/s measures the rate at which a parallel application can perform floating-point arithmetic operations. It is often used in scientific and engineering applications that involve intensive numerical calculations.

8. **I/O Throughput:** I/O throughput measures the rate at which data can be read from or written to storage devices. It is crucial for applications that handle large datasets or perform frequent I/O operations.

Performance Optimization:

Achieving optimal scalability and performance in parallel computing often involves a combination of algorithm design, efficient data distribution, load balancing, and minimizing communication overhead. Performance analysis tools and profiling can help identify bottlenecks and areas for improvement.

In summary, scalability and performance metrics are essential for assessing the efficiency and effectiveness of parallel applications. Evaluating scalability helps determine the ability to handle larger problems, while performance metrics provide quantifiable measures of resource utilization and computational efficiency. Effective performance optimization strategies are crucial for achieving high-performance computing in diverse application domains.

CHAPTER 3

Supercomputer Architecture

Supercomputers stand as the apex of computational power, pushing the boundaries of what is conceivable in the realm of computing. Within their colossal frames lie a symphony of processors, memory banks, and intricate interconnections, all working in unison to tackle the most challenging problems known to humanity. This chapter embarks on a journey into the heart of supercomputer architecture, where we unravel the intricacies of these extraordinary machines.

Unveiling the Computational Behemoths

Supercomputer architecture is a testament to human ingenuity in harnessing computational capabilities to solve complex problems. In this chapter, we'll delve into the very essence of these colossal machines. We'll explore the various architectural designs that underpin their exceptional performance, from clusters of processors to advanced accelerators. As we uncover the inner workings of supercomputers, you'll gain insights into how these architectural choices shape their capabilities and potential applications.

The Symphony of Processors and Memory

Central to the study of supercomputer architecture is the orchestration of processors and memory. These machines host a multitude of processing units, each with its own role in executing computations at unprecedented speeds. As we journey deeper, you'll discover the intricacies of parallel processing, where multiple processors collaborate harmoniously to tackle complex tasks simultaneously. We'll also delve into memory hierarchies, understanding how supercomputers manage vast amounts of data efficiently.

Interconnecting the Nodes

Supercomputers are not solitary entities but often interconnected clusters of processing nodes. The art of interconnection is a pivotal element of supercomputer design, allowing these systems to communicate seamlessly and distribute workloads effectively. In this chapter, we'll uncover the networks and topologies that underpin these interconnections, providing the essential lifelines that enable supercomputers to work as unified entities.

The Quest for Performance and Efficiency

Performance and energy efficiency are twin pursuits at the core of supercomputer architecture. We'll explore the innovations and techniques that supercomputer architects employ to extract every ounce of computational power while minimizing energy consumption. From advanced cooling systems to power-efficient designs, these machines are a testament to engineering excellence.

Applications as Vast as the Universe

The architectural choices made in supercomputers have a profound impact on the breadth of applications they can undertake. From simulating the behavior of subatomic particles to predicting climate patterns, from drug discovery to astrophysical simulations, supercomputers stand ready to tackle a vast array of scientific and engineering challenges.

Join us on this enlightening journey into the world of supercomputer architecture, where the boundaries of what is computationally achievable are continually expanded. Whether you are a seasoned computational scientist, an aspiring architect of supercomputing systems, or simply a curious explorer of cutting-edge technology, this chapter promises to reveal the remarkable inner workings of these computational behemoths. Supercomputer architecture is where innovation, engineering, and computational science converge to empower humanity to explore the frontiers of knowledge and discovery.

A. Cluster Supercomputers

Cluster supercomputers represent a prominent architectural

approach in the realm of high-performance computing (HPC). These computational powerhouses have gained immense popularity due to their scalability, cost-effectiveness, and ability to tackle a wide range of complex problems. In this exploration, we'll delve into the intricacies of cluster supercomputers, their architecture, benefits, and applications.

Cluster Supercomputer Architecture:

Cluster supercomputers are constructed by interconnecting multiple commodity off-the-shelf computers or servers, referred to as nodes. The architecture is based on the principle of distributed computing, where individual nodes collaborate to perform computations. Key elements of cluster supercomputer architecture include:

1. **Nodes:** Nodes in a cluster are individual computing units. These can be standard multi-core servers or workstations. The power of a cluster lies in the collective computational capability of these nodes.

2. **Interconnect:** Interconnects facilitate communication and data transfer among nodes. High-speed interconnects, such as InfiniBand or Ethernet with Remote Direct Memory Access (RDMA), are common choices to minimize latency and maximize data throughput.

3. **Networking:** Cluster nodes are connected through a network

infrastructure, which can be a high-speed local area network (LAN) or a dedicated high-performance network. High-bandwidth and low-latency networking are essential for efficient parallelism.

4. **Software Stack:** Cluster supercomputers rely on a robust software stack to manage and coordinate tasks across nodes. This includes job scheduling and resource management systems like Slurm or Torque, as well as parallel programming libraries and compilers.

Benefits of Cluster Supercomputers:

Cluster supercomputers offer several advantages, making them a preferred choice for a wide range of applications:

1. **Scalability:** Cluster architectures are highly scalable. As computational demands grow, additional nodes can be seamlessly integrated into the cluster, allowing organizations to expand their computing capabilities without major disruptions.

2. **Cost-Effectiveness:** Using commodity hardware reduces the cost of building and maintaining a cluster compared to specialized supercomputing systems. This makes HPC more accessible to a broader range of organizations.

3. **Flexibility:** Clusters are versatile and can be customized to

suit specific application requirements. Different nodes within a cluster can be tailored for various tasks, optimizing performance for different workloads.

4. **Parallelism:** Cluster supercomputers excel at parallel processing, making them suitable for a wide range of scientific simulations, data analysis, and engineering applications that benefit from distributing tasks across multiple nodes.

5. **Reliability:** Redundancy and fault-tolerant designs can be implemented in clusters to ensure high availability. If one node fails, the rest of the cluster can continue working.

Applications of Cluster Supercomputers:

Cluster supercomputers find applications in various fields due to their versatility and computational power:

1. **Scientific Research:** They are used extensively in scientific simulations, including climate modeling, astrophysics, nuclear physics, and molecular dynamics simulations.

2. **Engineering:** Engineers use cluster supercomputers for finite element analysis, computational fluid dynamics, and structural simulations to optimize product designs and improve performance.

3. **Data Analysis:** Cluster computing is employed in big data analytics, machine learning, and artificial intelligence to

process and analyze vast datasets.

4. **Genomics and Drug Discovery:** In genomics research and drug discovery, cluster supercomputers aid in DNA sequencing, protein folding simulations, and virtual screening of potential drug candidates.

5. **Weather Forecasting:** Weather prediction models rely on cluster supercomputers to perform complex simulations and deliver accurate forecasts.

6. **Academic and Educational Institutions:** Many universities and research institutions use cluster supercomputers for a wide range of scientific and computational research projects.

In summary, cluster supercomputers represent a flexible and cost-effective approach to high-performance computing. Their architecture allows organizations to harness the combined processing power of multiple commodity nodes, making them suitable for diverse applications across various domains. As computational demands continue to grow, cluster supercomputers remain at the forefront of scientific discovery and technological innovation.

B. Vector Supercomputers

Vector supercomputers are a class of high-performance

computing (HPC) systems that have played a pivotal role in scientific and engineering research since their inception in the 1970s. These supercomputers are characterized by their unique vector processing architecture, which enables them to excel in a wide range of scientific simulations and data-intensive computations. In this exploration, we'll delve into the intricacies of vector supercomputers, their architecture, historical significance, and applications.

Vector Supercomputer Architecture:

Vector supercomputers are distinguished by their vector processing units and memory subsystems, designed to efficiently perform mathematical operations on arrays of data. Key elements of vector supercomputer architecture include:

1. **Vector Registers:** Vector processors are equipped with specialized vector registers capable of holding large arrays of data elements. These registers enable parallel processing of vectorized instructions, resulting in efficient computation.

2. **Vector Pipelines:** Vector processors feature pipelines optimized for vectorized operations. These pipelines can process multiple data elements in parallel, dramatically increasing computational throughput.

3. **Memory Hierarchy:** Vector supercomputers typically have a memory hierarchy that includes fast vector registers, high-

speed cache memory, and main memory. This hierarchy minimizes data access latency, ensuring that the vector processors are constantly fed with data.

4. **Vector Instructions:** Vector processors execute vectorized instructions, such as addition or multiplication, on entire arrays of data in a single operation. This contrasts with scalar processors that operate on individual data elements.

5. **Vector Length:** The vector length is a critical parameter in vector supercomputers, representing the number of data elements that can be processed simultaneously in a vector operation. Longer vectors result in higher computational throughput.

6. **Vectorization Compiler:** Software development for vector supercomputers often involves writing code that can be efficiently vectorized by compilers. These compilers transform scalar code into vectorized instructions to leverage the full potential of the hardware.

Historical Significance:

Vector supercomputers have played a crucial role in advancing scientific research and computational capabilities:

1. **Cray-1 (1976):** The Cray-1, designed by Seymour Cray, is one of the earliest vector supercomputers. It set the standard

for vector processing and was used in various scientific fields, including weather prediction and nuclear simulations.

2. **Cray-2 (1985):** The Cray-2 introduced liquid cooling and improved vector processing capabilities. It was widely used in applications like computational fluid dynamics and computational chemistry.

3. **Cray X-MP (1982):** The Cray X-MP was one of the first supercomputers to offer multiple vector processors, further enhancing its computational power.

4. **NEC SX Series:** Japanese manufacturer NEC developed the SX series of vector supercomputers, which were used in weather forecasting, material science, and other research areas.

Applications of Vector Supercomputers:

Vector supercomputers have made significant contributions to various scientific and engineering fields:

1. **Weather Forecasting:** Vector supercomputers are instrumental in running numerical weather prediction models, providing accurate and timely forecasts.

2. **Astronomy and Astrophysics:** They are used for simulating celestial phenomena, galaxy formation, and the behavior of stars.

3. **Material Science:** Vector supercomputers aid in simulating the properties and behavior of materials under various conditions, essential for materials design and discovery.

4. **Fluid Dynamics:** Applications include simulating aerodynamics, turbulence, and fluid flow in engineering and aeronautics.

5. **Nuclear Simulations:** Vector supercomputers are employed in nuclear physics for simulating atomic nuclei and nuclear reactions.

6. **Molecular Dynamics:** Researchers use vector supercomputers to simulate the behavior of molecules and atoms, crucial for drug discovery and chemistry research.

7. **Particle Physics:** Vector supercomputers contribute to simulating particle interactions and data analysis in high-energy physics experiments.

In summary, vector supercomputers have made significant contributions to scientific and engineering research due to their unique vector processing architecture. While they have been supplemented by parallel computing models like clusters and GPUs, vector supercomputers remain relevant for specific applications that require high computational throughput and the processing of large datasets. They continue to drive innovation and exploration in various scientific disciplines, providing invaluable tools for researchers worldwide.

C. Massively Parallel Processing (MPP) Systems

Massively Parallel Processing (MPP) systems represent a powerful class of high-performance computing (HPC) systems designed to handle vast computational workloads by distributing and parallelizing tasks across a large number of processing nodes. MPP systems are known for their scalability, fault tolerance, and ability to deliver exceptional computational power. In this exploration, we'll delve into the intricacies of MPP systems, their architecture, advantages, and notable applications.

MPP System Architecture:

MPP systems are characterized by their architecture, which is designed to harness the combined processing power of a multitude of processing nodes. Key elements of MPP system architecture include:

1. **Processing Nodes:** The foundation of MPP systems lies in their processing nodes. These nodes are individual computing units, often commodity servers or specialized processors, interconnected within the MPP system. Each node contributes to the parallel execution of tasks.

2. **Interconnect:** Interconnection networks in MPP systems play

a critical role in facilitating high-speed communication and data transfer between processing nodes. These networks are designed for low latency and high bandwidth to ensure efficient parallelism.

3. **Distributed Memory:** Unlike shared-memory architectures, where all nodes have access to a common memory pool, MPP systems typically have distributed memory. Each processing node has its own memory, and communication between nodes is achieved through message passing.

4. **Parallel File System:** MPP systems often incorporate parallel file systems optimized for storing and accessing large volumes of data in parallel. These file systems are crucial for data-intensive applications.

5. **Software Stack:** The software stack in MPP systems includes job scheduling and resource management systems, parallel programming libraries, compilers, and specialized software for distributed computing. Message passing interfaces like MPI (Message Passing Interface) are commonly used for communication between nodes.

Advantages of MPP Systems:

MPP systems offer several advantages that make them well-suited for a wide range of applications:

1. **Scalability:** MPP systems are highly scalable, allowing organizations to expand their computing capabilities by adding more processing nodes. This scalability makes them suitable for handling both small and large computational workloads.

2. **Parallel Processing:** MPP systems excel at parallel processing, enabling the efficient distribution of tasks across numerous nodes. This makes them suitable for applications that require massive parallelism, such as scientific simulations and data analysis.

3. **Fault Tolerance:** MPP systems are designed with fault tolerance mechanisms to ensure uninterrupted operation even in the presence of hardware failures. Redundancy and failover strategies are commonly implemented.

4. **High Throughput:** MPP systems deliver high computational throughput, making them ideal for applications that demand significant computational power, such as weather modeling, numerical simulations, and data-intensive analytics.

5. **Customization:** Organizations can tailor MPP systems to meet specific application requirements. Different nodes can be optimized for various tasks, allowing for flexibility and performance optimization.

Applications of MPP Systems:

MPP systems find applications in diverse fields, thanks to their computational capabilities:

1. **Scientific Simulations:** MPP systems are used for simulating physical and natural phenomena, including climate modeling, astrophysical simulations, and fluid dynamics.

2. **Data Analytics:** MPP systems are employed for big data analytics, enabling organizations to process and analyze vast datasets for insights and decision-making.

3. **Genomics and Bioinformatics:** MPP systems aid in DNA sequencing, protein folding simulations, and genome analysis for advances in genomics research and drug discovery.

4. **Financial Modeling:** In the finance industry, MPP systems are used for risk analysis, portfolio optimization, and high-frequency trading algorithms.

5. **Energy Exploration:** MPP systems assist in seismic data processing for oil and gas exploration, optimizing drilling operations and reservoir modeling.

6. **Manufacturing and Engineering:** MPP systems are applied to finite element analysis, structural simulations, and computational fluid dynamics in manufacturing and engineering fields.

In summary, Massively Parallel Processing (MPP) systems are a class of high-performance computing systems that excel in parallelism and scalability. Their architecture, designed for distributing tasks across a multitude of processing nodes, makes them indispensable for a wide range of applications, from scientific simulations to data analytics and beyond. As computational demands continue to grow, MPP systems remain at the forefront of innovation and discovery across various domains.

D. Accelerated Computing: GPUs and FPGAs

Accelerated computing represents a paradigm shift in high-performance computing (HPC) and data processing. It leverages specialized hardware, such as GPUs and FPGAs, alongside traditional CPUs to dramatically increase computational power and efficiency. In this exploration, we'll delve into the intricacies of accelerated computing, the architecture of GPUs and FPGAs, their advantages, and notable applications.

GPU Architecture:

1. Streaming Multiprocessors (SMs): GPUs consist of multiple streaming multiprocessors (SMs), each containing a group of CUDA (Compute Unified Device Architecture) cores. These cores are responsible for executing parallel instructions, making GPUs highly efficient for parallel processing tasks.

2. Memory Hierarchy: GPUs feature a memory hierarchy that includes global memory, shared memory, and local memory. Global memory serves as the primary storage for data, while shared memory is used for communication between threads within the same thread block. Local memory is the slowest and is used as a fallback when other memory is exhausted.

3. Thread Blocks and Grids: In GPU programming, threads are organized into thread blocks, and multiple thread blocks form a grid. This hierarchical organization allows for efficient synchronization and parallelism.

4. SIMD Execution: GPUs employ Single Instruction, Multiple Data (SIMD) execution, meaning that a single instruction is executed across multiple data elements in parallel. This makes GPUs particularly well-suited for data-parallel workloads.

5. Parallelism: GPUs excel at parallelism and are capable of executing thousands of threads concurrently. They are commonly used in applications that require high-throughput parallel processing, such as scientific simulations, deep learning, and 3D rendering.

FPGA Architecture:

1. Configurability: FPGAs are highly configurable hardware devices. Unlike CPUs and GPUs, which have fixed instruction sets, FPGAs can be programmed to implement custom logic circuits and perform specific tasks.

2. Look-Up Tables (LUTs): FPGAs consist of an array of Look-Up Tables (LUTs) that can be configured to perform logic functions. These LUTs can be reprogrammed to implement various algorithms and computations.

3. Interconnects: FPGAs feature a network of programmable interconnects that allow different logic elements to be connected in various ways. This flexibility enables designers to create custom data paths and optimize performance.

4. Parallelism: FPGAs offer fine-grained parallelism, allowing for the concurrent execution of multiple operations. This makes them suitable for applications with intricate data dependencies and custom data processing pipelines.

5. Low Latency: FPGAs can achieve low-latency processing as they can be tailored to specific tasks. This is advantageous for applications that require real-time data processing, such as signal processing and hardware acceleration.

Advantages of Accelerated Computing:

1. Parallelism: Accelerated computing platforms, especially GPUs and FPGAs, are highly parallel and can process large datasets and complex computations much faster than traditional CPUs.

2. Energy Efficiency: GPUs and FPGAs are often more power-efficient than CPUs when it comes to parallel workloads, making them attractive for both performance and energy savings.

3. Customization: FPGAs, in particular, offer a high degree of customization. They can be tailored to specific tasks, which is valuable in applications where standard CPUs or GPUs may not be as efficient.

4. Performance Boost: Accelerated computing can provide a significant performance boost for a wide range of applications, including scientific simulations, machine learning, cryptography, and real-time data processing.

Applications of Accelerated Computing:

1. Deep Learning: GPUs are widely used in training deep neural networks due to their parallel processing capabilities. They have revolutionized the field of artificial intelligence and machine learning.

2. Scientific Simulations: Accelerated computing platforms are employed in scientific simulations, including molecular dynamics, climate modeling, and fluid dynamics simulations.

3. Cryptography: GPUs and FPGAs are used for cryptographic tasks, such as encryption, decryption, and hash function calculations, which require fast and efficient processing.

4. Real-Time Signal Processing: FPGAs are well-suited for real-time signal processing applications, such as radar, sonar, and image processing.

5. High-Frequency Trading: Financial institutions use GPUs for high-frequency trading algorithms, where low-latency processing is critical.

6. Image and Video Processing: GPUs are employed in image and video processing tasks, including video encoding, rendering, and computer vision applications.

In summary, accelerated computing with GPUs and FPGAs represents a powerful approach to achieving high-performance and energy-efficient processing for a wide range of applications. These specialized hardware platforms continue to drive innovation and advances in various fields, enabling faster and more efficient data analysis, simulations, and computations.

E. Quantum Supercomputers and Exotic Architectures

Quantum supercomputers and exotic architectures represent cutting-edge frontiers in high-performance computing (HPC) and computational technology. These extraordinary systems promise to revolutionize computing by harnessing quantum mechanics or unconventional physical principles to perform computations that are currently infeasible for classical computers. In this exploration, we'll delve into the intricacies of quantum supercomputers and exotic architectures, their unique features, advantages, and potential applications.

Quantum Supercomputers:

1. Quantum Bits (Qubits): Quantum supercomputers are built on the fundamental unit of quantum information, the qubit. Unlike classical bits, which can be either 0 or 1, qubits can exist in multiple states simultaneously, thanks to superposition. This property enables quantum computers to process vast amounts of data in parallel.

2. Entanglement: Another quantum property crucial to quantum computing is entanglement. Qubits can become entangled, meaning the state of one qubit is dependent on the state of another, regardless of the physical distance separating them. This property allows quantum computers to perform complex operations and solve problems that classical computers struggle with.

3. Quantum Gates: Quantum computations are executed using quantum gates that manipulate qubits. These gates include Hadamard gates, CNOT gates, and more. They enable quantum computers to perform operations like quantum parallelism and quantum interference, which underlie quantum algorithms.

4. Quantum Algorithms: Quantum computers are designed to run quantum algorithms that leverage quantum properties to solve problems efficiently. Examples include Shor's algorithm for factorizing large numbers and Grover's algorithm for searching unsorted databases.

5. Quantum Supremacy: Quantum supremacy is a term used to describe the point at which quantum computers can outperform the most advanced classical computers in specific tasks. Achieving quantum supremacy is a milestone in the development of quantum computing.

Exotic Architectures:

Exotic architectures refer to unconventional computing systems that are designed to harness specialized physical phenomena or principles for computation. Some notable examples include:

1. Optical Computing: Optical computing uses photons (light particles) instead of electrons to perform computations. Optical computing has the potential for ultra-fast data transfer and parallel processing due to the speed of light. It is explored for applications in telecommunications and encryption.

2. Neuromorphic Computing: Neuromorphic computing is inspired by the human brain's architecture and function. It uses artificial neural networks to perform tasks like pattern recognition and decision-making. Neuromorphic chips are designed to mimic the brain's parallel processing and energy efficiency.

3. DNA Computing: DNA computing leverages the properties of DNA molecules for computation. It is particularly useful for solving complex combinatorial problems and DNA-related tasks, such as sequence alignment and DNA-based computing devices.

4. Quantum Annealing: Quantum annealers are specialized quantum devices designed to solve optimization problems. They exploit quantum tunneling and thermal annealing to find the global minimum of a complex energy landscape.

5. Memristor-Based Computing: Memristors are novel electronic components that can change their resistance based on the history of applied voltage. They are explored for use in non-volatile memory and neuromorphic computing due to their potential for low-power, high-density storage and computing.

Advantages and Potential Applications:

Quantum Supercomputers:

1. **Cryptanalysis:** Quantum computers have the potential to break widely used encryption algorithms, prompting the need for post-quantum cryptography.

2. **Drug Discovery:** Quantum computers can simulate complex molecular interactions, accelerating drug discovery and

development.

3. **Optimization:** Quantum computers can optimize solutions for a wide range of problems, from logistics and supply chain management to financial portfolio optimization.

4. **Quantum Machine Learning:** Quantum computing can enhance machine learning algorithms, enabling more accurate predictions and pattern recognition.

Exotic Architectures:

1. **Neuromorphic Computing:** Neuromorphic chips can be used for real-time artificial intelligence applications, such as autonomous vehicles and robotics.

2. **Optical Computing:** Optical computing has applications in high-speed data transmission, optical character recognition, and image processing.

3. **DNA Computing:** DNA computing can be applied to solving NP-complete problems in areas like genomics and bioinformatics.

4. **Quantum Annealing:** Quantum annealers are valuable for solving optimization problems in fields like materials science and finance.

5. **Memristor-Based Computing:** Memristor-based computing

has potential applications in non-volatile memory, neuromorphic computing, and energy-efficient computing.

In summary, quantum supercomputers and exotic architectures represent pioneering frontiers in computing technology. Quantum supercomputers leverage the principles of quantum mechanics to perform computations that were previously considered infeasible. Exotic architectures harness unconventional physical phenomena to enable new computing paradigms and applications. These advancements have the potential to revolutionize industries, from cryptography and drug discovery to artificial intelligence and materials science, opening doors to unprecedented computational capabilities.

CHAPTER 4

High-Performance Computing (HPC) Technologies

In the ever-expanding landscape of computation, there exists a realm where raw processing power knows no bounds, where complex simulations unfold in the blink of an eye, and where the boundaries of human understanding are relentlessly pushed. Welcome to the world of High-Performance Computing (HPC) Technologies, a chapter in the grand saga of computing that explores the cutting-edge tools, techniques, and systems that empower us to solve the most intricate problems in science, engineering, research, and beyond.

Unveiling the Pinnacle of Computational Power

High-Performance Computing (HPC) is not merely a tool; it's a beacon of human innovation and an enabler of monumental discovery. This chapter serves as your guide through the heart of HPC, revealing the technologies that drive the engines of supercomputers, clusters, and accelerators. We'll unravel the mysteries of parallelism and scalability, delve into exotic architectures, and explore the quantum realm. HPC Technologies is a voyage into the heart of computational excellence, where computation is not just a task but an art form.

Mastering Supercomputing

The Symphony of Components

HPC Technologies is a symphony composed of hardware, software, and algorithms. We'll dissect the processing units, the intricate interconnects that bind them together, and the memory hierarchies that store vast amounts of data. We'll examine the software stacks that orchestrate computations and the algorithms that transform data into insights. This is where the orchestration of components gives birth to computational marvels.

Performance Beyond Imagination

HPC is a realm where performance transcends the ordinary. We'll explore how parallel processing and distributed architectures unleash the latent power of computation, tackling problems that were once deemed insurmountable. From clusters that form the backbone of scientific research to accelerators that redefine the meaning of speed, HPC Technologies is a journey into the realms of unprecedented computational might.

Applications as Vast as the Cosmos

In the world of HPC, the applications span the spectrum of human endeavor. Whether it's simulating the behavior of galaxies, predicting the intricate dance of subatomic particles, optimizing engineering marvels, or decoding the mysteries of the human genome, HPC is the compass guiding us through the uncharted territories of knowledge.

Join us in this exploration of High-Performance Computing (HPC) Technologies, where the pursuit of computational excellence meets the boundaries of human ingenuity. Whether you are a scientist pushing the boundaries of discovery, an engineer crafting the future, or simply an enthusiast of cutting-edge technology, this chapter promises to unveil the inner workings of the computational marvels that shape our world. In the world of HPC, the possibilities are limitless, and the journey is boundless.

A. High-Performance Interconnects

High-performance interconnects are the vital lifelines that connect the various components of supercomputers and high-performance computing (HPC) clusters, enabling seamless communication and data exchange among processing nodes. These interconnects play a pivotal role in determining the overall performance, scalability, and efficiency of HPC systems. In this exploration, we'll delve into the intricacies of high-performance interconnects, their architecture, significance, technologies, and real-world applications.

Architecture of High-Performance Interconnects:

High-performance interconnects are designed to provide low-latency and high-bandwidth communication between processing nodes. Key elements of high-performance interconnect architecture include:

1. **Topologies:** Interconnects are often built using various network topologies, including fat-tree, hypercube, torus, and mesh, among others. The choice of topology depends on factors such as scalability, fault tolerance, and communication patterns.

2. **Switches and Routers:** Interconnect networks incorporate switches and routers to manage data traffic efficiently. These devices determine how data is routed between processing nodes and can be configured for minimal latency and maximum throughput.

3. **InfiniBand and Ethernet:** InfiniBand and Ethernet are popular technologies used for high-performance interconnects. InfiniBand, in particular, is known for its low latency and high bandwidth, making it a preferred choice for HPC systems.

4. **Remote Direct Memory Access (RDMA):** RDMA technology enables direct memory-to-memory communication between processing nodes without involving the CPU. This reduces latency and CPU overhead, enhancing overall system performance.

5. **Redundancy:** High-performance interconnects often incorporate redundancy to ensure fault tolerance. Multiple paths and switches can be used to maintain system integrity in the event of hardware failures.

Significance of High-Performance Interconnects:

The performance and efficiency of HPC systems heavily depend on the quality of their interconnects:

1. **Low Latency:** Low-latency interconnects minimize the time it takes for data to travel between processing nodes. This is critical for applications that require real-time or near-real-time processing, such as simulations and scientific research.

2. **High Bandwidth:** High-bandwidth interconnects enable the rapid transfer of large volumes of data, making them suitable for data-intensive applications like big data analytics and machine learning.

3. **Scalability:** Scalable interconnects allow HPC systems to grow by adding more processing nodes without compromising performance. This scalability is essential for accommodating increasingly complex computational workloads.

4. **Message Passing:** Many HPC applications use message passing for communication between nodes. Efficient interconnects with support for message passing interfaces like MPI (Message Passing Interface) are crucial for parallelism.

5. **Energy Efficiency:** Energy-efficient interconnects help reduce power consumption in HPC systems, which is a critical consideration given the energy demands of large-scale

computing clusters.

Technologies and Real-World Applications:

High-performance interconnects find applications in various fields and technologies:

1. **Scientific Simulations:** Interconnects are crucial for running complex scientific simulations in fields like astrophysics, climate modeling, and nuclear physics, where massive data exchange is required.

2. **Financial Modeling:** High-frequency trading and risk analysis in finance rely on low-latency interconnects to process market data in real-time.

3. **Machine Learning:** Deep learning frameworks use high-bandwidth interconnects to distribute neural network training across multiple nodes in HPC clusters.

4. **Weather Forecasting:** High-performance interconnects support the rapid exchange of meteorological data for accurate and timely weather predictions.

5. **Drug Discovery:** Molecular modeling and drug discovery benefit from efficient interconnects to simulate molecular interactions and screen potential drug candidates.

6. **Oil and Gas Exploration:** Seismic data processing in the

energy industry depends on interconnects to analyze vast datasets for oil and gas exploration.

7. **Automotive and Aerospace Engineering:** Simulations for vehicle and aircraft design require interconnects to optimize performance and safety.

In summary, high-performance interconnects are the backbone of HPC systems, enabling fast and efficient communication among processing nodes. These interconnects are essential for a wide range of applications that demand low latency, high bandwidth, and scalability. As HPC continues to advance, high-performance interconnects will play an increasingly pivotal role in pushing the boundaries of computational research and discovery.

B. High-Performance Storage Systems

High-performance storage systems are the backbone of modern computing environments, especially in fields that require fast and efficient access to large volumes of data. These systems are designed to meet the growing demands of high-performance computing (HPC), big data analytics, scientific simulations, and other data-intensive applications. In this exploration, we'll delve into the intricacies of high-performance storage systems, their architecture, significance, technologies, and real-world applications.

Architecture of High-Performance Storage Systems:

High-performance storage systems employ advanced architectural designs to deliver speed, scalability, and reliability. Key elements of their architecture include:

1. **Parallel File Systems:** High-performance storage often relies on parallel file systems, which distribute data across multiple storage devices or nodes. This parallelization enables concurrent data access and boosts overall throughput.

2. **Storage Controllers:** Storage controllers manage data access and storage devices. They may include RAID (Redundant Array of Independent Disks) controllers for redundancy and fault tolerance.

3. **Storage Tiers:** High-performance storage systems often employ tiered storage architectures, where data is categorized based on access frequency and importance. Frequently accessed data is stored on high-speed storage media, while less frequently accessed data may reside on slower, high-capacity storage.

4. **Caching:** Caching mechanisms, such as read and write caches, are employed to accelerate data access. Frequently used data is temporarily stored in high-speed cache memory for rapid retrieval.

5. **Network Connectivity:** High-performance storage systems are connected to the compute nodes via high-speed, low-latency interconnects, such as InfiniBand or high-speed Ethernet. These connections ensure that data can flow seamlessly between storage and computing resources.

Significance of High-Performance Storage Systems:

High-performance storage systems are essential for various reasons:

1. **Reduced Latency:** These systems offer low-latency access to data, critical for applications that require real-time processing, like financial trading, scientific simulations, and gaming.

2. **High Throughput:** High-performance storage delivers high data throughput rates, making it ideal for processing and analyzing large datasets in fields such as genomics, weather modeling, and machine learning.

3. **Scalability:** Scalable storage architectures can expand to accommodate growing data volumes, ensuring that organizations can meet their data storage needs as they evolve.

4. **Fault Tolerance:** High-performance storage systems often incorporate redundancy and data protection mechanisms to ensure data integrity and availability, even in the event of hardware failures.

5. **Data Management:** These systems often include advanced data management features, such as data replication, snapshots, and data deduplication, to streamline data organization and backup.

Technologies and Real-World Applications:

High-performance storage systems are used across various fields and technologies:

1. **HPC and Scientific Computing:** These systems support scientific simulations, weather modeling, and nuclear research by providing fast access to massive datasets.

2. **Big Data Analytics:** High-performance storage is crucial for processing and analyzing big data, enabling organizations to derive valuable insights from vast datasets.

3. **Genomics and Bioinformatics:** In genomics research, high-performance storage accelerates DNA sequencing and analysis, contributing to advances in personalized medicine and genetics.

4. **Media and Entertainment:** High-performance storage is used in movie production, video editing, and real-time rendering for gaming to ensure fast access to high-resolution media files.

5. **Oil and Gas Exploration:** High-performance storage systems

facilitate the processing of seismic data and reservoir simulations in the energy sector.

6. **Financial Services:** In high-frequency trading and risk analysis, low-latency storage systems are vital for processing market data quickly and accurately.

7. **Aerospace and Automotive Engineering:** Simulations for vehicle and aircraft design rely on high-performance storage for efficient data access.

In conclusion, high-performance storage systems are essential components of modern computing environments, enabling fast and efficient access to vast amounts of data. These systems play a pivotal role in a wide range of applications, from scientific research and big data analytics to entertainment and industry-specific simulations. As data continues to grow in complexity and volume, high-performance storage systems will remain critical for meeting the demands of data-intensive computing.

C. Advanced Computing Tools and Libraries

Advanced computing tools and libraries are the unsung heroes of high-performance computing (HPC) and scientific research. They empower scientists, engineers, and researchers to harness the full potential of supercomputers and clusters, allowing them to simulate complex phenomena, analyze massive datasets, and solve intricate problems efficiently. In this exploration, we'll delve into the intricacies of advanced computing tools and libraries, their importance, key features, and real-world applications.

Importance of Advanced Computing Tools and Libraries:

1. **Productivity:** Advanced computing tools and libraries streamline the development process by providing pre-built functions and utilities. This accelerates the creation of complex applications, reducing development time and costs.

2. **Optimization:** These tools and libraries are optimized for high-performance computing environments, allowing researchers to make the most of the computational resources available to them.

3. **Scalability:** Advanced computing tools and libraries are designed to scale seamlessly across multiple processing nodes, ensuring that applications can take full advantage of parallelism in supercomputing clusters.

4. **Portability:** Many tools and libraries are designed to be cross-platform, making it easier for researchers to move their workloads between different HPC systems.

5. **Community Support:** These tools often have active user communities and forums, providing a wealth of knowledge and support for users.

Key Features of Advanced Computing Tools and Libraries:

1. **Parallel Programming Support:** Many libraries provide interfaces and functions for parallel programming, enabling developers to write applications that efficiently use multiple CPU cores or GPUs.

2. **Numerical Libraries:** Numerical libraries like BLAS (Basic Linear Algebra Subprograms) and LAPACK (Linear Algebra Package) provide a rich set of functions for linear algebra operations, making them essential for scientific computing.

3. **Message Passing Interfaces:** Libraries like MPI (Message Passing Interface) allow applications to communicate and coordinate tasks across multiple processing nodes in distributed computing environments.

4. **Visualization Tools:** Visualization libraries help researchers create meaningful representations of their data, aiding in the interpretation of complex results.

5. **Machine Learning Frameworks:** Some libraries include machine learning frameworks that enable researchers to develop and train AI models on HPC systems.

6. **Data Management and I/O:** Tools for efficient data management, including high-performance I/O libraries, are essential for handling large datasets in scientific simulations.

Real-World Applications:

1. **Climate Modeling:** Advanced computing tools and libraries enable scientists to simulate climate models, helping us understand climate change and its impacts.

2. **Astrophysics:** Researchers use these tools to analyze astronomical data, model the behavior of celestial bodies, and simulate cosmic phenomena.

3. **Drug Discovery:** In pharmaceutical research, advanced computing tools assist in simulating molecular interactions and drug candidate screening, expediting drug discovery.

4. **Materials Science:** Tools and libraries are used to simulate the properties of materials at the atomic and molecular levels, aiding in the development of new materials for various applications.

5. **Aeronautics and Aerospace:** Advanced computing tools play a crucial role in simulating and optimizing aircraft designs and spacecraft trajectories.

6. **Energy Research:** Tools are used in simulations related to nuclear energy, fusion, and renewable energy sources to study and optimize energy production.

7. **Genomics:** Researchers in genomics and bioinformatics rely on these tools for sequence analysis, structural biology, and

population genetics.

8. **Financial Modeling:** In the financial sector, advanced computing tools and libraries are used for risk analysis, portfolio optimization, and algorithmic trading.

In conclusion, advanced computing tools and libraries are indispensable for scientific research, engineering simulations, and various applications in HPC. They empower researchers to unlock the full potential of supercomputing resources, accelerate discoveries, and address complex challenges across a wide range of domains. As computational demands continue to grow, the development and enhancement of these tools will remain essential for advancing science and technology.

D. In-Memory Computing

In-memory computing is a revolutionary paradigm in the field of data processing and computing architecture. It leverages the speed and efficiency of main memory (RAM) to perform data storage and processing tasks, bypassing the limitations of traditional disk-based storage systems. In this exploration, we'll delve into the intricacies of in-memory computing, its significance, key features, and real-world applications.

Significance of In-Memory Computing:

In-memory computing addresses critical challenges in data processing and analytics:

1. **Speed:** In-memory computing systems are significantly faster than traditional disk-based systems because data is stored in RAM, allowing for near-instantaneous data access.

2. **Real-Time Analytics:** In-memory computing enables real-time or near-real-time analytics, making it suitable for applications where timely insights are crucial, such as financial trading and fraud detection.

3. **Complex Analytics:** It supports complex data processing tasks, including complex queries, machine learning, and graph analytics, without the bottlenecks associated with disk I/O.

4. **Scalability:** In-memory systems can easily scale by adding more RAM or nodes to accommodate growing data volumes and processing demands.

Key Features of In-Memory Computing:

1. **In-Memory Data Storage:** Data is loaded into RAM, where it remains readily accessible for processing. This eliminates the need to fetch data from slower disk storage.

2. **Distributed Computing:** Many in-memory computing

platforms support distributed computing, enabling parallel processing across multiple nodes for high scalability.

3. **Low Latency:** In-memory computing systems offer ultra-low latency, making them ideal for applications requiring immediate responses, such as e-commerce and gaming.

4. **In-Memory Databases:** In-memory databases, like SAP HANA and Redis, are built around in-memory computing principles and provide fast and efficient data storage and retrieval.

5. **Data Persistence:** Some in-memory systems provide options for data persistence, allowing data to be stored in-memory while periodically flushed to disk for durability.

Real-World Applications:

1. **Financial Services:** In-memory computing is widely used in high-frequency trading, risk analysis, and fraud detection. It enables the rapid analysis of market data and the identification of trading opportunities or anomalies.

2. **E-commerce:** In-memory computing powers recommendation engines, personalized content delivery, and real-time inventory management in e-commerce platforms.

3. **Telecommunications:** In the telecom industry, in-memory computing accelerates call processing, billing, and network

optimization tasks.

4. **Healthcare:** It supports real-time analysis of medical data, aiding in disease diagnosis, treatment optimization, and patient monitoring.

5. **Manufacturing:** In-memory computing is used for real-time monitoring and optimization of manufacturing processes, ensuring product quality and efficiency.

6. **Logistics and Supply Chain:** It optimizes route planning, demand forecasting, and inventory management in logistics and supply chain operations.

7. **Internet of Things (IoT):** In-memory computing facilitates real-time data processing in IoT applications, enabling the rapid response to sensor data and device commands.

8. **Big Data Analytics:** In-memory technologies are integrated into big data platforms like Apache Spark and Apache Flink, enhancing their performance for real-time and batch analytics.

9. **Scientific Research:** In-memory computing is used in scientific simulations and data analysis, allowing researchers to process and analyze large datasets quickly.

In conclusion, in-memory computing is a game-changer in the world of data processing and analytics. Its ability to leverage the speed of main memory for storage and processing tasks has revolutionized real-time analytics, high-frequency trading, and numerous other applications across various industries. As data volumes continue to grow, in-memory computing will remain a crucial technology for unlocking the full potential of data-driven insights and real-time decision-making.

E. Energy Efficiency in HPC

Energy efficiency in High-Performance Computing (HPC) is a critical concern as supercomputers and data centers continue to grow in scale and complexity. These energy-efficient practices are essential for reducing operational costs, minimizing environmental impact, and addressing the power consumption challenges associated with running large HPC clusters. In this exploration, we'll delve into the intricacies of energy efficiency in HPC, its significance, key strategies, and real-world applications.

Significance of Energy Efficiency in HPC:

Energy efficiency is a pressing concern in the HPC community for several reasons:

1. **Cost Savings:** HPC systems consume massive amounts of electricity, and reducing energy consumption can result in significant cost savings, especially for large-scale data centers.

2. **Environmental Impact:** Energy-intensive computing can

have a substantial carbon footprint. Energy-efficient HPC helps mitigate this impact, aligning with sustainability goals and regulations.

3. **Sustainable Growth:** As HPC continues to advance, managing power consumption is crucial for sustaining the growth of computing capabilities within power and thermal constraints.

4. **Operational Stability:** Efficient cooling and power distribution are essential for maintaining the reliability and operational stability of HPC clusters.

Key Strategies for Energy Efficiency in HPC:

1. **Optimized Hardware:** Selecting energy-efficient components, such as CPUs, GPUs, and memory, is essential. Modern processors often incorporate power-saving features like dynamic voltage and frequency scaling (DVFS).

2. **Efficient Cooling:** Data centers employ advanced cooling solutions, such as hot/cold aisle containment, liquid cooling, and free cooling, to maintain optimal temperatures while reducing energy consumption.

3. **Energy-Aware Scheduling:** Job schedulers in HPC clusters can optimize resource allocation to minimize power usage. Tasks can be assigned to nodes with the most energy-efficient

hardware.

4. **Dynamic Voltage and Frequency Scaling (DVFS):** DVFS adjusts the voltage and frequency of processors based on workload, reducing power consumption during periods of low demand.

5. **Idle Node Management:** Turning off or idling nodes when they are not in use can significantly reduce energy consumption. Wake-on-LAN and intelligent power management tools help with this.

6. **Energy Monitoring and Analytics:** Real-time energy monitoring and data analytics enable administrators to identify power-hungry components and inefficient configurations for optimization.

7. **Energy-Efficient Algorithms:** Developing and implementing energy-efficient algorithms can reduce computational requirements and, consequently, energy consumption.

8. **Renewable Energy Integration:** Data centers are exploring the use of renewable energy sources, such as solar and wind power, to reduce their reliance on fossil fuels.

Real-World Applications:

1. **Weather and Climate Modeling:** Energy-efficient HPC systems are used to simulate and predict weather patterns and

assess climate change impacts. These models are crucial for disaster preparedness and environmental research.

2. **Pharmaceutical Research:** Energy-efficient HPC accelerates drug discovery and molecular modeling, leading to more efficient research in healthcare.

3. **Aerospace Engineering:** The aerospace industry relies on HPC for aircraft design and simulation. Energy efficiency is crucial for optimizing fuel consumption and emissions.

4. **Automotive Industry:** Energy-efficient HPC systems help automotive manufacturers simulate crash tests, aerodynamics, and fuel efficiency, leading to safer and more fuel-efficient vehicles.

5. **Energy Sector:** HPC assists in energy exploration, reservoir simulations, and grid optimization, contributing to the efficient generation and distribution of energy.

6. **Financial Services:** High-frequency trading relies on energy-efficient HPC clusters for rapid market analysis and decision-making.

7. **Academic Research:** Energy-efficient HPC benefits various academic disciplines, from physics and chemistry to social sciences, by providing researchers with computational power while minimizing environmental impact.

In conclusion, energy efficiency in HPC is a multifaceted challenge that requires a combination of hardware optimization, cooling strategies, intelligent management, and renewable energy integration. As HPC continues to play a crucial role in scientific research, industry, and academia, energy-efficient practices will remain a top priority for organizations seeking to balance computational capabilities with sustainability goals.

CHAPTER 5

Supercomputing Software Stack

In the realm of supercomputing, where the boundaries of computational capability are constantly pushed to new frontiers, the software that orchestrates the immense power of these machines plays a pivotal role. The Supercomputing Software Stack is the digital symphony that harmonizes the complex interplay of hardware components, enabling scientists, engineers, and researchers to tackle some of the most challenging problems known to humanity. In this chapter, we embark on a journey through the layers of the Supercomputing Software Stack, exploring its critical components, functions, and the transformative impact it has on the world of high-performance computing (HPC).

Engineering the Miraculous

The Supercomputing Software Stack is a testament to human ingenuity, where innovation converges with necessity. It is a carefully orchestrated ensemble of operating systems, programming models, libraries, and frameworks designed to harness the raw power of supercomputers. It serves as a bridge between the intricate architecture of these computing giants and the diverse applications that seek to unveil the secrets of the universe, simulate natural phenomena, and solve the most complex problems humanity faces.

From Bare Hardware to Boundless Potential

At its core, the Supercomputing Software Stack transforms bare hardware into a computational behemoth. It breathes life into processors, memory, and storage, giving birth to a system that can perform billions of calculations per second. This chapter is a journey into the depths of this transformative process, from the foundational layers of operating systems and programming models to the libraries and frameworks that unlock the potential of parallelism, enabling breakthroughs in scientific discovery and engineering marvels.

Exploring the Uncharted Territories

Throughout this exploration, we will unravel the mysteries of supercomputing software, uncovering the secrets behind parallelism, message passing, and the efficient orchestration of computational workflows. We will discover how these components facilitate scientific simulations, weather predictions, drug discoveries, and a host of other applications that redefine what is possible in the world of computing.

Join us on this voyage through the Supercomputing Software Stack, where innovation and computation converge to tackle some of the greatest challenges humanity has ever faced. Whether you are a seasoned HPC professional, a researcher pushing the boundaries of discovery, or simply an enthusiast of cutting-edge technology, this chapter promises to reveal the inner workings of the software that drives the computational marvels shaping our world. In the realm of supercomputing, the possibilities are boundless, and the journey is one of perpetual discovery.

A. HPC Operating Systems

High-Performance Computing (HPC) operating systems are the unsung heroes of the supercomputing world. These specialized operating systems are engineered to harness the full potential of HPC hardware, providing the foundation upon which scientific simulations, data analyses, and complex computations unfold. In this exploration, we'll delve into the intricacies of HPC operating systems, their significance, key features, and real-world applications.

Significance of HPC Operating Systems:

HPC operating systems are of paramount importance in the following ways:

1. **Efficiency:** HPC operating systems are fine-tuned for performance, ensuring that every resource within the computing cluster is optimized for speed and parallelism.

2. **Scalability:** They are designed to scale efficiently across thousands or even millions of processing cores, enabling scientists and engineers to tackle monumental computational tasks.

3. **Resource Management:** HPC operating systems excel in resource allocation and management, allowing multiple users and jobs to share the computing infrastructure seamlessly.

4. **Parallelism:** They facilitate the execution of parallel workloads, exploiting multicore processors, accelerators like GPUs, and high-speed interconnects to accelerate computations.

5. **Reliability:** Reliability is paramount in HPC, where computational errors can be costly. HPC operating systems prioritize stability to ensure long-running simulations proceed without interruption.

Key Features of HPC Operating Systems:

1. **Lightweight Kernels:** Many HPC operating systems employ lightweight kernel designs that reduce overhead and latency. Examples include the Linux kernel and specialized lightweight kernels like CNK (Compute Node Kernel).

2. **Job Scheduling:** HPC operating systems incorporate job schedulers like Slurm and Torque, which efficiently allocate

computing resources to user tasks based on priority and availability.

3. **Parallel File Systems:** These systems integrate parallel file systems like Lustre and GPFS (IBM Spectrum Scale) to provide high-speed, distributed storage capable of handling massive datasets.

4. **Message Passing Libraries:** MPI (Message Passing Interface) libraries are often bundled with HPC operating systems, facilitating interprocess communication for parallel applications.

5. **Cluster Management Tools:** HPC operating systems include tools like OpenHPC and Bright Cluster Manager for streamlined cluster setup, configuration, and monitoring.

6. **Containerization:** Container technologies like Docker and Singularity are integrated into some HPC operating systems to simplify application deployment and management.

Real-World Applications:

1. **Scientific Research:** HPC operating systems power simulations in fields like astrophysics, climate modeling, nuclear physics, and materials science, enabling groundbreaking discoveries.

2. **Engineering Simulations:** Aerospace, automotive, and civil

engineering rely on HPC systems to simulate designs, test prototypes, and optimize performance.

3. **Pharmaceuticals:** Drug discovery, molecular modeling, and protein folding simulations are accelerated by HPC operating systems, expediting advancements in healthcare.

4. **Weather Forecasting:** HPC clusters process vast amounts of meteorological data to generate accurate and timely weather forecasts, aiding disaster preparedness.

5. **Energy Sector:** HPC is instrumental in optimizing energy production, reservoir simulations, and grid management in the energy sector.

6. **Financial Services:** High-frequency trading and risk analysis in finance depend on HPC systems for rapid data processing and analysis.

7. **Genomics and Bioinformatics:** HPC operating systems support genomic sequencing, structural biology, and personalized medicine research.

In conclusion, HPC operating systems are the bedrock upon which the world's most advanced computations are built. They empower researchers, engineers, and scientists to unravel complex problems, unlock new scientific frontiers, and drive technological innovation. As the demand for computational power continues to grow, HPC operating systems will remain essential for pushing the boundaries of what is computationally possible.

B. Programming Models in HPC: MPI, OpenMP, and CUDA

High-Performance Computing (HPC) applications are often complex and computationally intensive, requiring efficient ways to harness the power of supercomputers and parallel processing. Programming models provide the foundation for developing software that can exploit the parallelism and capabilities of HPC hardware. In this exploration, we'll delve into the intricacies of three critical programming models: MPI (Message Passing Interface), OpenMP, and CUDA. Each of these models serves specific purposes in the HPC ecosystem and enables developers to create efficient, parallel, and high-performance applications.

MPI (Message Passing Interface):

Significance of MPI:

MPI is a widely used programming model for distributed memory systems in HPC. It facilitates communication and coordination between processes running on separate nodes within a cluster. The significance of MPI lies in its ability to enable parallelism in distributed memory systems, allowing scientists and engineers to solve large-scale problems efficiently.

Key Features of MPI:

1. **Message Passing:** MPI provides a standardized set of functions and procedures for processes to exchange messages, making it ideal for parallel applications that require inter-process communication.

2. **Portability:** MPI is available on various HPC platforms and is supported by multiple programming languages, including C, C++, and Fortran, ensuring portability across different systems.

3. **Scalability:** MPI applications can scale to thousands or even millions of processing cores, making it suitable for large-scale simulations and computations.

4. **Collective Operations:** MPI supports collective operations like broadcast, scatter, gather, and reduce, enabling efficient data sharing and synchronization among processes.

5. **Point-to-Point Communication:** Developers can create custom communication patterns using point-to-point communication routines, allowing for flexibility in message passing.

OpenMP:

Significance of OpenMP:

OpenMP is a programming model for shared-memory systems, often used in multi-core processors and symmetric multiprocessing (SMP) systems. It simplifies parallel programming by providing a set of directives that allow developers to specify which parts of the code should run in parallel.

Key Features of OpenMP:

1. **Directive-Based Parallelism:** OpenMP introduces compiler directives, such as "#pragma omp," that guide the compiler in parallelizing code sections. This approach simplifies the development of multi-threaded applications.

2. **Task Parallelism:** OpenMP supports task parallelism, allowing developers to express parallelism at a high level by defining tasks and dependencies.

3. **Worksharing Constructs:** Developers can use worksharing constructs like "parallel for" and "parallel sections" to parallelize loops and sections of code, distributing the workload across multiple threads.

4. **Thread Management:** OpenMP handles thread creation, management, and synchronization, making it easier for

developers to write parallel code.

5. **Portability:** OpenMP is supported by many compilers and is available in multiple programming languages, including C, C++, and Fortran.

CUDA (Compute Unified Device Architecture):

Significance of CUDA:

CUDA is a programming model developed by NVIDIA for parallel computing on GPUs (Graphics Processing Units). It has gained prominence in various fields, including scientific simulations, deep learning, and computational finance, due to the massively parallel nature of GPUs.

Key Features of CUDA:

1. **Massive Parallelism:** CUDA unlocks the parallel processing power of GPUs, which consist of thousands of cores, enabling high-throughput computations.

2. **CUDA C/C++ Language:** Developers can write CUDA code using extensions to standard C/C++ languages, allowing them to create custom GPU kernels and manage data transfers between CPU and GPU memory.

3. **GPU Libraries:** CUDA provides libraries like cuBLAS (for linear algebra), cuDNN (for deep learning), and cuFFT (for

Fast Fourier Transforms), offering optimized GPU-accelerated functions.

4. **Unified Memory:** CUDA introduces unified memory, simplifying data management by allowing both the CPU and GPU to access the same memory address space.

5. **Dynamic Parallelism:** With dynamic parallelism, GPU kernels can launch other GPU kernels, enabling more flexible and intricate parallelism.

Real-World Applications:

1. **MPI:** MPI is crucial for large-scale scientific simulations, weather modeling, and quantum chemistry calculations that require distributed memory systems.

2. **OpenMP:** OpenMP is commonly used in tasks such as image processing, video encoding, and numerical simulations, benefiting from shared-memory parallelism on multi-core processors.

3. **CUDA:** CUDA is indispensable for deep learning, scientific simulations, and real-time image processing, leveraging the massive parallelism of GPUs for speed and efficiency.

In conclusion, these programming models, MPI, OpenMP, and CUDA, are foundational for HPC, enabling developers to harness the full potential of parallel processing, whether it's in distributed memory systems, shared-memory multi-core processors, or GPU-accelerated computing. These models empower researchers and engineers to tackle complex problems and drive innovations in various scientific and industrial domains.

C. Compilers and Debugging Tools in High-Performance Computing (HPC)

Compilers and debugging tools are the unsung heroes of high-performance computing (HPC). These software components bridge the gap between human-readable code and machine-executable instructions, ensuring that HPC applications run efficiently, reliably, and without errors. In this exploration, we'll delve into the intricacies of compilers and debugging tools, their significance, key features, and real-world applications within the HPC ecosystem.

Significance of Compilers and Debugging Tools in HPC:

1. **Performance Optimization:** Compilers are essential for transforming high-level code into optimized machine code that fully utilizes the potential of HPC hardware, including multi-core processors and accelerators like GPUs.

2. **Debugging and Error Detection:** Debugging tools are critical for identifying and fixing errors and inefficiencies in HPC applications, ensuring their reliability and accuracy.

3. **Parallelism and Vectorization:** Compilers play a pivotal role in parallelizing code and vectorizing operations, enabling efficient utilization of computational resources in HPC clusters.

4. **Portability:** Compilers and debugging tools facilitate code portability across different HPC platforms, allowing developers to target various architectures without extensive code modifications.

5. **Heterogeneous Computing:** In the era of heterogeneous computing, debugging tools assist in diagnosing issues in code that combines CPU and GPU computations.

Key Features of Compilers:

1. **Optimization Techniques:** Compilers employ a range of optimization techniques, including loop optimization, function inlining, and auto-vectorization, to enhance the performance of HPC applications.

2. **Parallelization:** Compiler directives, such as OpenMP and CUDA, enable developers to specify parallelism in the code, allowing for efficient execution on multi-core processors and GPUs.

3. **Target Architectures:** Compilers are designed to target specific architectures, optimizing code generation for CPUs,

GPUs, and other accelerators commonly used in HPC.

4. **Interoperability:** They provide mechanisms for interoperability between different languages, such as C, C++, and Fortran, enabling developers to use libraries and tools in their preferred languages.

Key Features of Debugging Tools:

1. **Breakpoint and Watchpoints:** Debugging tools allow developers to set breakpoints in their code and watch variables, enabling step-by-step execution and inspection of program state.

2. **Memory Analysis:** Tools like Valgrind and Intel Inspector help identify memory leaks, buffer overflows, and other memory-related issues that can lead to application crashes.

3. **Profiling:** Profiling tools provide insights into code performance, highlighting bottlenecks and areas for optimization by measuring execution time, memory usage, and resource utilization.

4. **Parallel Debugging:** For parallel and distributed applications, debugging tools support the analysis of complex interactions between multiple processes or threads.

5. **Reverse Debugging:** Some advanced tools allow developers to rewind and replay program execution, helping diagnose

intermittent issues.

Real-World Applications:

1. **Climate Modeling:** HPC applications in climate modeling rely on compilers to optimize complex mathematical simulations. Debugging tools assist in identifying errors and ensuring the accuracy of climate predictions.

2. **Aerospace Engineering:** Compilers and debugging tools are essential for optimizing software used in aerospace engineering simulations, such as finite element analysis for structural design.

3. **Biomedical Research:** HPC applications in genomics, drug discovery, and protein folding benefit from compiler optimizations and debugging tools to accelerate research.

4. **Energy Sector:** Compilers and debugging tools are used in simulations for oil and gas reservoir management and the optimization of renewable energy sources.

5. **Quantum Computing:** For quantum computing simulations, compilers are employed to generate code for quantum processors, and debugging tools aid in troubleshooting complex quantum algorithms.

6. **Financial Services:** In high-frequency trading and risk analysis, compiler optimizations and debugging tools ensure

the reliability and speed of financial models.

In conclusion, compilers and debugging tools are indispensable in the world of HPC, enabling developers to create high-performance applications, identify and fix errors, and optimize code for a wide range of applications. These tools play a vital role in advancing scientific research, engineering simulations, and data-intensive computations across various domains. As computational demands continue to grow, compilers and debugging tools will remain essential for achieving efficient and reliable HPC solutions.

D. HPC Libraries and Frameworks

High-Performance Computing (HPC) libraries and frameworks are the backbone of computational science and engineering. They provide pre-built, optimized functions, routines, and tools that empower researchers and developers to leverage the full potential of supercomputers and high-performance clusters. In this exploration, we'll delve into the intricacies of HPC libraries and frameworks, their significance, key features, and real-world applications within the HPC ecosystem.

Significance of HPC Libraries and Frameworks:

1. **Efficiency:** HPC libraries and frameworks are meticulously optimized for performance, ensuring that computations can

make the most of the available hardware resources, including multi-core processors, GPUs, and high-speed interconnects.

2. **Productivity:** They accelerate application development by providing pre-built functions and routines, reducing development time and the likelihood of errors.

3. **Portability:** HPC libraries and frameworks are often designed to be cross-platform, ensuring that code can be deployed on different HPC systems with minimal modifications.

4. **Parallelism:** These tools facilitate parallel programming by offering parallel algorithms and data structures, simplifying the exploitation of parallel processing capabilities.

5. **Interoperability:** HPC libraries and frameworks can interface with various programming languages, enabling developers to leverage existing code and integrate it into their HPC applications.

Key Features of HPC Libraries:

1. **Numerical Computing:** Libraries like BLAS (Basic Linear Algebra Subprograms), LAPACK (Linear Algebra Package), and FFTW (Fastest Fourier Transform in the West) provide a rich set of functions for numerical computing, essential for scientific simulations.

2. **Parallel Programming:** Libraries like MPI (Message Passing

Interface) and OpenMP offer interfaces and functions for parallel programming, enabling developers to write applications that efficiently use multiple CPU cores or GPUs.

3. **Data Manipulation:** Libraries like HDF5 (Hierarchical Data Format) and NetCDF (Network Common Data Form) facilitate data storage and manipulation, crucial for handling large datasets in scientific simulations.

4. **Machine Learning and Deep Learning:** Libraries like TensorFlow, PyTorch, and scikit-learn offer machine learning and deep learning capabilities, enabling HPC applications to integrate AI-driven components.

Key Features of HPC Frameworks:

1. **Workflow Management:** HPC frameworks like Apache Airflow and Pegasus enable the creation, execution, and management of complex computational workflows, orchestrating multiple tasks and data dependencies.

2. **Distributed Computing:** Frameworks like Apache Spark and Apache Hadoop provide distributed computing capabilities, allowing for the processing of massive datasets across clusters of machines.

3. **Containerization:** Frameworks like Singularity and Docker facilitate the encapsulation of HPC applications and their

dependencies into containers, simplifying deployment and reproducibility.

4. **Cluster Management:** Frameworks like Slurm and Torque are used for cluster and job management, ensuring efficient resource allocation and job scheduling on HPC systems.

Real-World Applications:

1. **Weather Forecasting:** HPC libraries are used in numerical weather models to simulate atmospheric conditions and improve weather forecasts.

2. **Materials Science:** Computational chemistry and materials science heavily rely on HPC libraries for simulating molecular interactions and properties of materials.

3. **Astrophysics:** Libraries and frameworks aid in simulating celestial bodies, gravitational interactions, and the behavior of the universe.

4. **Aeronautics and Aerospace:** HPC libraries and frameworks are used in simulations for aircraft design, aerodynamics, and spacecraft trajectories.

5. **Genomics:** HPC libraries and frameworks support genomics research by enabling sequence analysis, structural biology simulations, and population genetics studies.

6. **Oil and Gas Exploration:** Libraries and frameworks are employed for reservoir simulations, optimizing oil and gas exploration and production.

7. **Financial Services:** HPC libraries and frameworks accelerate risk analysis, portfolio optimization, and algorithmic trading in the financial sector.

In conclusion, HPC libraries and frameworks are indispensable tools for scientific research, engineering simulations, and data-intensive computations. They empower developers and researchers to accelerate discoveries, solve complex problems, and advance knowledge across various domains. As the demand for computational power continues to grow, the development and enhancement of these tools will remain essential for unlocking the full potential of HPC resources.

E. Workflow Management in Supercomputing

In the world of supercomputing, where complex simulations, data analyses, and scientific research projects involve an intricate sequence of tasks, workflow management plays a pivotal role. Workflow management systems are the orchestration engines that streamline and automate the execution of computational workflows on supercomputers and high-performance computing (HPC) clusters. In this exploration, we'll delve into the intricacies of workflow management in supercomputing, its significance, key features, and real-world applications.

Significance of Workflow Management in Supercomputing:

1. **Efficiency:** Workflow management systems automate and optimize the execution of tasks, reducing manual intervention and minimizing idle time on supercomputers. This leads to more efficient resource utilization.

2. **Reproducibility:** Workflows ensure that complex experiments and simulations are executed consistently, making it easier to reproduce results, validate research findings, and collaborate with other researchers.

3. **Scalability:** Workflow management systems can scale to handle large-scale simulations and data-intensive tasks by distributing workloads across multiple nodes or even supercomputers.

4. **Resource Allocation:** They provide mechanisms for allocating computing resources, scheduling jobs, and monitoring job progress, facilitating effective resource management in HPC environments.

Key Features of Workflow Management in Supercomputing:

1. **Graphical Interfaces:** Many workflow management systems

offer graphical interfaces for designing workflows visually. Users can define tasks, dependencies, and data flows using a drag-and-drop interface.

2. **Scripting and Automation:** Advanced users can script workflows using domain-specific languages or scripting languages like Python. This allows for fine-grained control and customization.

3. **Dependency Management:** Workflows define dependencies between tasks, ensuring that each task is executed only when its prerequisites are satisfied. This prevents unnecessary computation.

4. **Data Management:** Workflow management systems handle data input and output, including data staging, data transfer, and data archiving. They ensure that data is available when needed and moved efficiently.

5. **Fault Tolerance:** In large-scale computations, failures can occur. Workflow management systems incorporate fault tolerance mechanisms to handle errors gracefully, such as task retries or alternative task execution.

6. **Parallel Execution:** Workflows can include parallel tasks, enabling the execution of multiple tasks concurrently on supercomputing clusters with many cores.

Real-World Applications:

1. **Scientific Simulations:** Workflow management is vital in scientific fields such as computational chemistry, astrophysics, and climate modeling, where complex simulations involve a sequence of tasks with dependencies.

2. **Bioinformatics:** Genomic research relies on workflow management systems to automate sequence analysis, genome assembly, and variant calling, handling large datasets efficiently.

3. **Drug Discovery:** Pharmaceutical companies use workflows to automate high-throughput screening, molecular modeling, and drug candidate selection, accelerating drug discovery processes.

4. **Engineering Simulations:** Aerospace and automotive industries employ workflow management for aerodynamics simulations, structural analysis, and crash testing, streamlining design and testing procedures.

5. **Weather Forecasting:** Meteorological agencies use workflows to automate weather model runs, data assimilation, and ensemble forecasting, improving the accuracy and timeliness of weather predictions.

6. **Financial Modeling:** In quantitative finance, workflows

automate tasks like risk assessment, portfolio optimization, and algorithmic trading, enabling timely decision-making.

7. **Energy Sector:** Oil and gas companies use workflows for reservoir simulations, seismic data processing, and drilling optimization, supporting efficient energy exploration.

In conclusion, workflow management in supercomputing is a crucial enabler of scientific discovery, engineering innovation, and data-intensive research. These systems facilitate the orchestration of complex tasks, ensuring efficiency, reproducibility, and scalability in HPC environments. As supercomputing continues to drive advancements across various domains, workflow management will remain an indispensable tool for researchers and engineers seeking to unlock the full potential of computational resources.

CHAPTER 6

Supercomputing Applications

Supercomputing, with its unprecedented computational power, opens the door to a realm of possibilities that were once considered unattainable. In the chapter on Supercomputing Applications, we embark on a journey through the diverse and impactful landscapes where supercomputers are deployed to tackle some of the most complex and pressing challenges of our time. From simulating the birth of stars to unraveling the mysteries of the human genome, supercomputing applications span a multitude of domains, each driven by the pursuit of knowledge, innovation, and transformation.

Unleashing the Computational Titans

Supercomputing applications represent the pinnacle of computational science and engineering, where problems that were once thought insurmountable are now approached with confidence and precision. This chapter delves into the fascinating worlds of scientific discovery, engineering innovation, and data-driven insights, highlighting how supercomputers are transforming industries, accelerating research, and shaping the future of technology.

From the Cosmic to the Molecular

Supercomputing applications are as diverse as the universe itself. In these pages, we explore the cosmic wonders of astrophysics and cosmology, where supercomputers simulate the evolution of galaxies and the dynamics of black holes. We venture into the intricate realm of molecular biology, where supercomputers decipher the genetic code, accelerate drug discovery, and pave the way for personalized medicine.

Impact Across Industries

Beyond the realms of science, supercomputing extends its reach to industries such as aerospace, automotive, and energy, where simulations refine designs, optimize fuel efficiency, and unlock sustainable energy sources. We delve into the financial sector, where supercomputing algorithms drive high-frequency trading and risk analysis, shaping the global economy. From weather prediction to climate modeling, supercomputing provides the tools to safeguard lives and mitigate the impact of natural disasters.

Infinite Possibilities

The applications of supercomputing are as limitless as human curiosity. As we navigate the diverse landscapes of supercomputing applications, we witness the profound impact of these computational giants on our world. Whether you are a scientist pushing the boundaries of knowledge, an engineer redefining what's possible, or simply curious about the boundless potential of supercomputing, this chapter promises to unveil the awe-inspiring applications that are shaping the future of our world. Supercomputing, it turns out, is not just about computing; it's about expanding the horizons of what we can achieve.

A. Scientific Simulations and Modeling

Scientific simulations and modeling represent a transformative intersection of science, mathematics, and high-performance computing (HPC). These techniques have become essential tools for researchers across various domains, enabling them to explore complex phenomena, simulate natural processes, and make predictions that would be impossible or impractical to achieve through traditional experimentation alone. In this exploration, we'll delve into the intricacies of scientific simulations and modeling, their significance, methodologies, and real-world applications across scientific disciplines.

Significance of Scientific Simulations and Modeling:

1. **Exploration of Complex Phenomena:** Scientific simulations allow researchers to investigate complex, multifaceted phenomena that are challenging to study experimentally, such as astrophysical events, fluid dynamics in turbulent flows, or biological processes at the molecular level.

2. **Hypothesis Testing:** Modeling and simulation provide a means to test hypotheses and theories, allowing researchers to refine their understanding of natural phenomena, validate existing theories, or even propose new ones.

3. **Predictive Power:** Simulations offer predictive capabilities, enabling scientists to forecast the behavior of systems in response to various conditions. This has applications in weather forecasting, climate modeling, and material science, among others.

4. **Resource Efficiency:** In some cases, conducting experiments in the physical world can be costly, dangerous, or environmentally unsustainable. Simulations offer a more efficient and ethical alternative.

Methodologies of Scientific Simulations and Modeling:

1. **Mathematical Models:** Scientific simulations begin with the formulation of mathematical models that describe the underlying physical, chemical, or biological processes. These models often take the form of differential equations, which capture how quantities change over time.

2. **Numerical Methods:** To transform mathematical models into computational simulations, numerical methods are employed. These methods discretize continuous equations into discrete time steps and spatial grids, allowing for iterative calculations.

3. **Parallel Computing:** High-performance computing (HPC) is crucial for scientific simulations, as many complex models require extensive computational resources. Parallel computing techniques, such as MPI (Message Passing Interface) and GPU acceleration, are commonly used to harness the power of supercomputers and clusters.

4. **Visualization and Analysis:** Visualization tools enable researchers to interpret simulation results, turning data into comprehensible images or animations. Data analysis techniques help extract meaningful insights from simulation output.

Real-World Applications:

1. **Astrophysics:** Simulations model celestial events, such as the formation of galaxies, the life cycles of stars, and the dynamics of black holes, aiding our understanding of the cosmos.

2. **Climate Modeling:** Climate models simulate interactions among the atmosphere, oceans, land, and ice to predict climate patterns, inform climate change policy, and assess the impact of global warming.

3. **Molecular Biology:** Molecular dynamics simulations explore the behavior of biological molecules like proteins and DNA, enabling drug discovery, understanding disease mechanisms, and protein folding studies.

4. **Material Science:** Computational materials science leverages simulations to design new materials with desired properties, advance semiconductor technology, and optimize structural materials for aerospace and automotive applications.

5. **Fluid Dynamics:** Simulations of fluid flow help optimize aircraft design, study the behavior of oceans and rivers, and improve combustion processes in engines.

6. **Nuclear Physics:** In nuclear physics, simulations model the behavior of subatomic particles, aiding in our understanding of fundamental forces and nuclear reactions.

7. **Earthquake Prediction:** Seismology simulations predict the effects of earthquakes, enhancing early warning systems and disaster preparedness.

In conclusion, scientific simulations and modeling have revolutionized research across diverse scientific disciplines, enabling scientists and researchers to explore the unknown, test hypotheses, and make predictions with remarkable precision. As computational capabilities continue to advance, these techniques will play an increasingly central role in pushing the boundaries of human knowledge and addressing some of the most pressing challenges facing our world today.

B. Weather and Climate Prediction

Weather and climate prediction, powered by high-performance computing (HPC), is a remarkable field at the intersection of atmospheric science, computer modeling, and data analysis. It enables us to forecast short-term weather conditions and long-term climate trends, providing critical information for disaster management, agriculture, energy planning, and policy decision-making. In this exploration, we'll delve into the intricacies of weather and climate prediction, their significance, methodologies, and real-world applications.

Significance of Weather and Climate Prediction:

1. **Disaster Preparedness:** Accurate weather forecasts are essential for early warning systems that help mitigate the impact of natural disasters, including hurricanes, tornadoes, floods, and wildfires.

2. **Agriculture:** Farmers rely on weather predictions for crop planning, irrigation, and pest control, optimizing yields and reducing losses.

3. **Energy Sector:** Energy companies use weather forecasts to manage energy demand, plan renewable energy generation, and optimize the operation of power grids.

4. **Aviation and Transportation:** Airlines, shipping companies, and transportation agencies depend on weather forecasts for

safe and efficient operations.

5. **Climate Policy:** Climate models and predictions inform international climate agreements and climate change mitigation efforts by providing insights into future climate trends.

Methodologies of Weather and Climate Prediction:

1. **Data Collection:** Weather prediction relies on vast networks of weather stations, satellites, radar systems, and ocean buoys that continuously collect data on temperature, humidity, wind speed, and other atmospheric variables.

2. **Numerical Weather Prediction (NWP):** NWP models simulate the atmosphere's behavior by dividing it into a grid and solving mathematical equations that describe physical processes like fluid dynamics and thermodynamics. These models are initialized with current observational data.

3. **Ensemble Forecasting:** Instead of relying on a single model, ensemble forecasting involves running multiple simulations with slight variations in initial conditions or model parameters. This approach provides a range of possible outcomes, enhancing forecast accuracy and confidence.

4. **Climate Models:** Climate models are more extensive and long-term simulations that project climate patterns over

decades to centuries. They consider factors like greenhouse gas emissions, ocean currents, and ice melt.

5. **High-Performance Computing:** HPC clusters and supercomputers are essential for running the complex simulations required for both NWP and climate modeling. These machines can process vast amounts of data and perform the necessary calculations quickly.

Real-World Applications:

1. **Hurricane Tracking:** Weather prediction models track the development and path of hurricanes, providing early warnings to residents in their path and enabling disaster preparedness.

2. **Crop Management:** Farmers use weather forecasts for planting and harvesting schedules, irrigation planning, and pest control, increasing agricultural productivity.

3. **Renewable Energy:** Wind and solar energy production are highly dependent on weather conditions. Forecasts help energy companies optimize power generation and grid management.

4. **Climate Change Projections:** Climate models predict future climate trends, informing policy decisions related to greenhouse gas emissions, sea-level rise, and adaptation strategies.

5. **Aviation Safety:** Airports and airlines rely on accurate weather forecasts to ensure passenger safety and minimize flight delays due to adverse weather conditions.

6. **Flood Control:** Weather forecasts help manage reservoirs and dams, reducing the risk of floods and ensuring the efficient use of water resources.

7. **Oceanography:** Climate models and ocean circulation simulations aid in understanding ocean behavior, including El Niño and La Niña events, which impact global weather patterns.

In conclusion, weather and climate prediction, empowered by advances in high-performance computing and data collection, have transformed our ability to anticipate and respond to atmospheric changes. These predictions are instrumental in safeguarding lives, enhancing economic resilience, and addressing global challenges like climate change. As technology continues to evolve, weather and climate prediction will only become more accurate and indispensable for a wide range of applications and policy decisions.

C. Computational Chemistry and Drug Discovery

Computational chemistry and drug discovery represent a

dynamic synergy of science, computer modeling, and high-performance computing (HPC). These fields are instrumental in accelerating the development of new pharmaceuticals, understanding molecular interactions, and designing drugs with higher precision. In this exploration, we'll delve into the intricacies of computational chemistry and drug discovery, their significance, methodologies, and real-world applications in the pharmaceutical industry and medical research.

Significance of Computational Chemistry and Drug Discovery:

1. **Speeding Drug Development:** Traditional drug discovery can be a lengthy and expensive process. Computational methods allow for the rapid screening of millions of potential drug candidates, significantly reducing development timelines.

2. **Cost Reduction:** By minimizing the need for physical experiments, computational chemistry saves pharmaceutical companies substantial costs associated with lab research and clinical trials.

3. **Precision Medicine:** Computational models enable the design of drugs tailored to individual patient characteristics, leading to more effective treatments with fewer side effects.

4. **Drug Repurposing:** Computational methods help identify

existing drugs that can be repurposed for new medical applications, potentially bypassing lengthy development phases.

5. **Understanding Molecular Interactions:** Computational chemistry provides insights into the interactions between drugs and biological molecules at the atomic and molecular levels, shedding light on their mechanisms of action.

Methodologies of Computational Chemistry and Drug Discovery:

1. **Molecular Modeling:** Computational chemists use molecular modeling techniques to create three-dimensional representations of molecules. This includes methods like molecular mechanics, quantum mechanics, and molecular dynamics simulations.

2. **Drug Screening:** Virtual screening involves the computational analysis of chemical databases to identify molecules with potential drug-like properties. This is done by evaluating factors such as binding affinity and pharmacokinetics.

3. **Protein-Ligand Docking:** Docking simulations predict how drug candidates bind to target proteins, providing insights into binding affinities and potential drug interactions.

4. **Quantum Chemistry:** Quantum chemistry calculations provide detailed information about molecular structures, electronic properties, and reaction mechanisms at the quantum level.

5. **Machine Learning and Artificial Intelligence:** AI and machine learning algorithms are increasingly used to analyze large datasets, predict drug-target interactions, and discover novel drug candidates.

6. **High-Performance Computing:** Drug discovery simulations, particularly molecular dynamics simulations, require massive computational power. HPC clusters and supercomputers are essential for conducting these simulations efficiently.

Real-World Applications:

1. **Drug Design:** Computational methods are used to design new drug candidates by predicting their chemical properties, binding affinity to target proteins, and potential side effects.

2. **Protein Folding:** Understanding protein folding is crucial for drug design. Computational models help predict protein structures and folding pathways, aiding in the development of therapies for protein misfolding diseases.

3. **Virtual Screening:** Computational screening identifies potential drug candidates from large chemical libraries,

narrowing down the list of compounds to be tested in laboratories.

4. **ADME Prediction:** Absorption, distribution, metabolism, and excretion (ADME) predictions help assess the pharmacokinetics of potential drugs, aiding in the selection of candidates with favorable properties.

5. **Toxicology Prediction:** Computational models assess the toxicity of drug candidates, reducing the risk of adverse effects during clinical trials.

6. **Drug Repurposing:** Computational methods identify existing drugs that could be effective in treating new diseases or conditions, speeding up drug development for emerging health threats.

7. **Personalized Medicine:** Computational approaches enable the customization of drug treatments based on individual genetic and molecular profiles, improving treatment efficacy and reducing side effects.

In conclusion, computational chemistry and drug discovery are revolutionizing the pharmaceutical industry by accelerating drug development, optimizing drug design, and facilitating the discovery of novel treatments. These fields are at the forefront of precision medicine, offering the potential to tailor therapies to individual patient needs and address some of the most pressing health challenges of our time. As computational tools and techniques continue to evolve, the future of drug discovery holds even greater promise for the development of innovative, effective, and personalized medicines.

D. Astrophysics and Space Exploration

Astrophysics and space exploration are captivating fields that delve into the mysteries of the cosmos, driven by scientific curiosity, technological advancement, and high-performance computing (HPC). These disciplines enable us to comprehend the universe's vastness, unravel celestial phenomena, and explore the potential for life beyond our planet. In this exploration, we'll delve into the intricacies of astrophysics and space exploration, their significance, methodologies, and their profound impact on our understanding of the cosmos and humanity's place within it.

Significance of Astrophysics and Space Exploration:

1. **Cosmic Understanding:** Astrophysics seeks to answer fundamental questions about the universe's origins, its evolution, the nature of dark matter and dark energy, and the existence of extraterrestrial life.

2. **Technological Advancement:** Space exploration drives technological innovation, leading to advancements in materials science, robotics, telecommunications, and

computing that benefit numerous industries on Earth.

3. **Earth Observation:** Space missions provide critical data on Earth's climate, weather, and natural disasters, contributing to environmental monitoring, disaster response, and resource management.

4. **Inspiration and Education:** Space exploration captivates the human imagination, inspiring generations of scientists, engineers, and dreamers. It serves as a powerful educational tool, fostering STEM (Science, Technology, Engineering, and Mathematics) interest and literacy.

Methodologies of Astrophysics and Space Exploration:

1. **Observational Astronomy:** Astronomers use ground-based telescopes, space observatories, and radio telescopes to collect data from celestial objects, studying light and other electromagnetic radiation emitted or reflected by stars, galaxies, and cosmic phenomena.

2. **Theoretical Astrophysics:** Theoretical astrophysicists develop mathematical models and simulations to understand the fundamental processes governing the universe, such as the behavior of stars, galaxies, black holes, and the expansion of the cosmos.

3. **Space Missions:** Space exploration involves the launch of

spacecraft and rovers to study celestial bodies and phenomena up close. Missions range from planetary exploration to deep space observatories like the Hubble Space Telescope.

4. **High-Performance Computing:** HPC plays a crucial role in astrophysics and space exploration by simulating complex cosmic phenomena, processing vast datasets, and aiding in spacecraft navigation and control.

Real-World Applications:

1. **Planetary Exploration:** Space missions like NASA's Mars rovers, Curiosity and Perseverance, explore the surface of Mars, searching for signs of past or present life and studying the planet's geology.

2. **Cosmic Observatories:** Telescopes like the Hubble Space Telescope and the James Webb Space Telescope provide breathtaking images and data on distant galaxies, nebulae, and exoplanets, expanding our understanding of the cosmos.

3. **Black Hole Research:** Observations and simulations of black holes, such as the Event Horizon Telescope's image of the supermassive black hole at the center of galaxy M87, shed light on these enigmatic objects and their role in galaxy formation.

4. **Exoplanet Discovery:** Space telescopes and ground-based

observatories have identified thousands of exoplanets, some of which may be suitable for life, revolutionizing our understanding of planetary systems beyond our solar system.

5. **Gravitational Waves:** The detection of gravitational waves, such as those from the merger of two black holes, confirms Einstein's theory of general relativity and opens a new era of astronomy, allowing the study of cosmic phenomena beyond the electromagnetic spectrum.

6. **Space Weather Monitoring:** Space missions and observations help monitor space weather, including solar flares and geomagnetic storms, which can impact satellite communications, GPS, and power grids on Earth.

In conclusion, astrophysics and space exploration stand at the forefront of scientific discovery, expanding our knowledge of the universe and inspiring humankind to reach for the stars. These disciplines push the boundaries of technology, deepen our understanding of the cosmos, and contribute to practical applications on Earth. As we continue to explore the cosmos and harness the power of HPC, we embark on a journey of discovery that reveals not only the mysteries of space but also our own place in the grand tapestry of the universe.

E. Engineering and Automotive Design

Engineering and automotive design are integral to shaping the modern world, driving innovation in transportation, manufacturing, and infrastructure. These fields, often empowered by high-performance computing (HPC), play a pivotal role in developing safe, efficient, and sustainable vehicles and systems. In this exploration, we'll delve into the intricacies of engineering and automotive design, their significance, methodologies, and real-world applications in revolutionizing mobility and transportation.

Significance of Engineering and Automotive Design:

1. **Transportation Advancement:** Automotive design innovations have transformed the way people and goods move, impacting not only personal mobility but also logistics, trade, and urban planning.

2. **Safety Enhancement:** Engineering solutions, such as advanced materials, crash-test simulations, and autonomous driving technologies, have contributed to making vehicles safer for passengers and pedestrians.

3. **Environmental Sustainability:** Automotive engineers are developing cleaner, more fuel-efficient, and electric vehicles to reduce greenhouse gas emissions and combat climate change.

4. **Technological Integration:** Modern vehicles are equipped with advanced electronics, sensors, and connectivity features, enhancing driver experience, safety, and efficiency.

Methodologies of Engineering and Automotive Design:

1. **Computer-Aided Design (CAD):** CAD software enables engineers to create detailed 2D and 3D models of vehicle components and systems, facilitating virtual prototyping and design optimization.

2. **Finite Element Analysis (FEA):** FEA simulations assess the structural integrity of vehicle components, predicting how they will perform under various loads and conditions, from crash tests to everyday use.

3. **Computational Fluid Dynamics (CFD):** CFD simulations analyze airflow around a vehicle, optimizing aerodynamics for fuel efficiency, reducing drag, and enhancing vehicle stability.

4. **Crash Testing and Safety Simulations:** Engineers use HPC for crash simulations, evaluating vehicle safety in different collision scenarios without physical prototypes.

5. **Materials Science:** Advances in materials science help develop lightweight, durable, and sustainable materials for vehicles, enhancing performance and fuel efficiency.

6. **Electric and Autonomous Vehicle Modeling:** Engineers

model electric powertrains and autonomous vehicle behavior, fine-tuning algorithms and assessing their safety and reliability.

Real-World Applications:

1. **Vehicle Design:** Automotive engineers use CAD and simulation tools to design vehicles that are aerodynamically efficient, structurally sound, and aesthetically pleasing.

2. **Crash Safety:** HPC simulations model crash scenarios, allowing engineers to design vehicles with optimal crumple zones and safety systems to protect occupants.

3. **Fuel Efficiency:** Computational simulations optimize engine design, reducing fuel consumption and emissions while maintaining performance.

4. **Electric Vehicles (EVs):** Engineers model and simulate EV components like batteries, motors, and charging systems to improve range, efficiency, and charging infrastructure.

5. **Autonomous Vehicles:** HPC supports the development of self-driving vehicles by simulating real-world scenarios, testing algorithms, and ensuring safety in a controlled virtual environment.

6. **Advanced Materials:** Computational modeling aids in the development of lightweight materials, composites, and

sustainable alternatives to traditional automotive materials.

7. **Vehicle Dynamics:** Engineers use simulations to optimize suspension systems, tire designs, and chassis configurations, improving vehicle handling and ride comfort.

8. **Aircraft and Aerospace:** Similar engineering and design principles apply to aircraft and spacecraft, from optimizing aerodynamics to ensuring structural integrity in extreme conditions.

In conclusion, engineering and automotive design are at the forefront of technological advancement, reshaping the transportation landscape and addressing pressing challenges such as climate change and road safety. With the aid of HPC and innovative design methodologies, engineers continue to push the boundaries of what is possible in vehicle design, promising a future of cleaner, safer, and more efficient mobility solutions for all.

CHAPTER 7

Supercomputing in Artificial Intelligence and Machine Learning

In the age of information, where data flows ceaselessly and the quest for intelligent machines becomes ever more compelling, the fusion of supercomputing with artificial intelligence (AI) and machine learning (ML) stands as a beacon of innovation. This chapter delves into the captivating convergence of supercomputing prowess and the intricacies of AI and ML, offering a glimpse into how these cutting-edge technologies are reshaping industries, unlocking scientific discoveries, and paving the way for a future where machines mimic human cognitive functions. From deep learning's computational hunger to the boundless possibilities of AI-driven scientific exploration, this chapter uncovers the intricate tapestry of supercomputing's role in shaping the intelligence of tomorrow.

Unleashing Computational Titans

Supercomputing, with its staggering computational power, emerges as the catalyst for AI and ML applications on an unprecedented scale. It equips researchers, data scientists, and engineers with the tools to crunch massive datasets, train intricate neural networks, and orchestrate the complex symphony of algorithms required to achieve artificial intelligence and machine learning's grand promises.

From Data to Intelligence

At the heart of this synergy lies the art of transforming raw data into actionable intelligence. Supercomputers accelerate this alchemical process, enabling machines to comprehend human language, recognize patterns, make predictions, and even delve into the depths of scientific inquiry. Whether in healthcare, finance, or scientific research, supercomputing empowers AI and ML to traverse uncharted territories of knowledge and innovation.

Challenges and Possibilities

Yet, with great computational power comes great responsibility and challenges. The chapter examines the computational demands of AI algorithms, the ethical considerations of machine learning, and the quest for energy-efficient supercomputing solutions. It also reveals the infinite possibilities for AI-driven scientific discovery, from drug design to particle physics, and the evolution of human-machine collaboration that is transforming the landscape of industry and research.

In a world where AI and ML are not just buzzwords but transformative forces, this chapter illuminates the dynamic relationship between supercomputing and intelligent machines. It invites you to explore the intricacies of these technologies, their impact on our lives, and the limitless horizons they continue to unveil. Supercomputing, when coupled with AI and ML, is not merely a tool; it's the forge where the future of intelligence is being shaped.

A. Deep Learning and Neural Network Training

Deep learning is a subfield of machine learning that has sparked a revolution in artificial intelligence (AI). It revolves around neural networks—complex computational models inspired by the human brain—capable of automatically learning and extracting patterns from data. This chapter explores the foundations, techniques, and real-world applications of deep learning, shedding light on how neural networks are trained and their pivotal role in modern AI.

Foundations of Deep Learning:

1. **Neural Networks:** At the core of deep learning are artificial neural networks, composed of interconnected layers of artificial neurons (nodes). These networks are designed to process and transform data in a hierarchical manner, mimicking the human brain's structure.

2. **Deep Architectures:** Deep learning earns its name from the depth of neural networks. Deep architectures, with many

hidden layers (deep layers), enable networks to learn intricate and abstract features from raw data, making them suitable for complex tasks.

3. **Activation Functions:** Activation functions, such as the rectified linear unit (ReLU) or sigmoid, introduce non-linearity to neural networks, enabling them to capture complex relationships in data.

Training Neural Networks:

1. **Backpropagation:** Neural networks learn through a process called backpropagation. During training, they adjust their internal parameters (weights and biases) iteratively to minimize the difference between predicted outputs and actual targets.

2. **Loss Functions:** Loss functions quantify the discrepancy between predicted and actual values. Training aims to minimize this loss, and different tasks (classification, regression, etc.) require specific loss functions.

3. **Optimization Algorithms:** Optimization algorithms, like stochastic gradient descent (SGD), Adam, or RMSprop, guide the adjustment of network parameters during training to reach the optimal values that minimize the loss.

4. **Mini-Batch Training:** Rather than using the entire dataset in

each training iteration, mini-batch training divides the data into smaller subsets (mini-batches), making training more efficient and allowing for faster convergence.

5. **Regularization Techniques:** Techniques like dropout and L1/L2 regularization prevent overfitting by reducing the complexity of the network and encouraging it to generalize better to unseen data.

Deep Learning Applications:

1. **Image Recognition:** Deep learning has excelled in image recognition tasks, including object detection, facial recognition, and image segmentation, with applications in autonomous vehicles, medical imaging, and security systems.

2. **Natural Language Processing (NLP):** In NLP, deep learning models like transformers have revolutionized tasks such as machine translation, sentiment analysis, and chatbots, enabling human-like language understanding.

3. **Recommendation Systems:** Deep learning powers recommendation algorithms used by platforms like Netflix and Amazon to suggest products and content to users based on their preferences.

4. **Healthcare:** Deep learning aids in medical image analysis, disease diagnosis, drug discovery, and predicting patient

outcomes, improving healthcare diagnostics and treatments.

5. **Autonomous Systems:** Deep learning is essential for self-driving cars, drones, and robotics, enabling these systems to perceive and interact with their environments.

6. **Finance:** Deep learning models are used in fraud detection, algorithmic trading, and risk assessment, enhancing decision-making and security in the financial sector.

Challenges and Future Directions:

1. **Data Quality and Quantity:** Deep learning models require vast amounts of high-quality labeled data for training, which can be a bottleneck in some applications.

2. **Interpretability:** Deep neural networks are often considered black boxes, making it challenging to understand how they arrive at their decisions—a critical concern in fields like healthcare and law.

3. **Compute Resources:** Training deep neural networks demands substantial computational power, driving the need for supercomputing and specialized hardware like GPUs and TPUs.

4. **Ethical and Bias Concerns:** Deep learning models can perpetuate biases present in training data, leading to ethical and fairness issues that demand careful consideration.

5. **Continual Learning:** Future research aims to develop techniques for lifelong learning, where models can adapt to new data and tasks without catastrophic forgetting.

In conclusion, deep learning and neural network training have revolutionized AI, enabling machines to tackle complex tasks with human-level performance. Their applications span across diverse domains, and ongoing research seeks to address challenges while unlocking new frontiers in AI capabilities. As deep learning continues to advance, its influence on technology and society is set to grow, shaping the future of AI-driven solutions.

B. AI-Driven Scientific Discovery

Artificial Intelligence (AI) has ushered in a transformative era in scientific research, accelerating the pace of discovery, optimizing experiments, and uncovering hidden insights in vast datasets. In this chapter, we'll delve into the dynamic intersection of AI and scientific discovery, exploring how machine learning, data analysis, and advanced algorithms are revolutionizing fields ranging from medicine and materials science to astronomy and genomics.

The Power of AI in Scientific Research:

1. **Data Processing and Analysis:** AI excels in processing large volumes of complex data, making it invaluable for analyzing

genomics data, particle physics data from colliders, astronomical observations, and more.

2. **Pattern Recognition:** Machine learning algorithms can detect subtle patterns in data that might elude human researchers, enabling the discovery of novel correlations and relationships.

3. **Automation of Experiments:** AI-driven robotics and autonomous systems can conduct experiments around the clock, drastically reducing the time needed for research.

4. **Predictive Modeling:** AI models can predict outcomes, helping researchers design experiments with a higher likelihood of success and efficiency.

AI in Scientific Fields:

1. **Drug Discovery:** AI is revolutionizing drug discovery by accelerating the identification of potential drug candidates, analyzing their safety and efficacy, and streamlining clinical trials.

2. **Materials Science:** AI-powered simulations and data analysis are aiding the development of advanced materials with properties tailored for specific applications, from aerospace to renewable energy.

3. **Genomics and Healthcare:** AI is driving genomic sequencing and analysis, leading to personalized medicine,

disease prediction, and drug development.

4. **Astronomy and Space Exploration:** AI algorithms assist in the analysis of astronomical data, identifying exoplanets, exploring cosmic phenomena, and improving space mission planning.

5. **Climate Science:** AI models help predict climate patterns, analyze climate data, and optimize renewable energy systems, contributing to climate change mitigation and adaptation.

Challenges and Future Directions:

1. **Interpretable AI:** Ensuring AI-driven insights are interpretable and explainable is crucial, especially in fields like healthcare where trust and accountability are paramount.

2. **Data Quality and Bias:** High-quality, unbiased data is essential for AI-driven scientific discovery. Addressing biases in data and AI models is an ongoing challenge.

3. **Data Privacy:** Balancing the need for data sharing and collaboration with privacy concerns is a complex issue, particularly in genomics and healthcare.

4. **Energy Efficiency:** AI-driven simulations and training can be computationally intensive. Developing energy-efficient AI algorithms and hardware is a priority.

5. **Cross-Disciplinary Collaboration:** Effective collaboration between AI experts and domain-specific scientists is essential for harnessing AI's full potential in scientific research.

6. **Ethical Considerations:** Ethical frameworks for AI in research, including issues of consent, data ownership, and responsible AI use, must be established.

Real-World Impact:

1. **Drug Discovery:** AI models have identified promising drug candidates for diseases like COVID-19, significantly speeding up the drug development process.

2. **Proteomics:** AI-driven proteomics is enhancing our understanding of protein structures and functions, with applications in drug design and disease research.

3. **Climate Modeling:** AI models are improving the accuracy of climate simulations, aiding in climate change predictions and policy decisions.

4. **Materials Discovery:** AI-driven materials discovery is leading to breakthroughs in energy storage, lightweight materials, and catalysis, with implications for renewable energy and industry.

5. **Space Exploration:** AI is optimizing space missions, such as the Mars rovers, by autonomously navigating and conducting

experiments on distant planets.

In conclusion, AI-driven scientific discovery is revolutionizing research across diverse fields, pushing the boundaries of human knowledge, and addressing some of the world's most pressing challenges. As AI continues to evolve and integrate with scientific methodologies, the future holds immense promise for groundbreaking discoveries and innovative solutions to complex problems. It's a thrilling era where AI is not just a tool but a driving force in expanding our understanding of the natural world.

C. Supercomputing for Big Data Analytics

In today's data-driven world, the ability to process, analyze, and derive insights from massive datasets is paramount. Supercomputing, with its unparalleled computational power, is playing a pivotal role in enabling organizations to tackle the challenges of big data analytics. This chapter explores how supercomputing is reshaping the landscape of big data, from scientific research and business intelligence to healthcare and finance.

The Significance of Supercomputing in Big Data Analytics:

1. **Handling Massive Volumes of Data:** Big data analytics involves processing and analyzing datasets of unprecedented size and complexity, which is beyond the capabilities of

conventional computing systems.

2. **Complex Algorithms:** Analyzing big data often requires complex algorithms, machine learning models, and simulations, which demand immense computational resources.

3. **Real-Time Analytics:** In some applications, such as financial trading or cybersecurity, real-time analytics are critical, necessitating rapid data processing and decision-making.

4. **Scientific Discovery:** In scientific research, supercomputing accelerates data analysis in fields like genomics, particle physics, and climate science, where datasets are massive and require complex simulations.

Supercomputing Techniques for Big Data Analytics:

1. **Parallel Processing:** Supercomputers leverage parallel processing capabilities, splitting tasks into smaller subtasks that can be executed simultaneously across multiple processing cores, dramatically reducing computation time.

2. **Distributed Computing:** Supercomputing clusters and grids distribute data and computational workloads across multiple interconnected nodes, allowing for efficient processing of large datasets.

3. **In-Memory Computing:** Supercomputers equipped with

large memory capacities enable in-memory processing, where data is stored in RAM for faster access and analysis.

4. **GPU Acceleration:** Graphics Processing Units (GPUs) are used to accelerate specific computations, such as deep learning and data-intensive tasks, significantly enhancing performance.

5. **High-Performance Storage:** Supercomputers are equipped with high-speed, high-capacity storage systems that can handle the rapid read/write operations required for big data analytics.

Applications of Supercomputing in Big Data Analytics:

1. **Scientific Research:** Supercomputing accelerates data analysis in fields like genomics, where DNA sequencing generates massive datasets for personalized medicine and disease research.

2. **Climate Modeling:** Climate scientists use supercomputers to analyze vast amounts of data for climate modeling, predicting weather patterns, and assessing the impact of climate change.

3. **Financial Services:** In the financial sector, supercomputing enables high-frequency trading, risk analysis, fraud detection, and portfolio optimization through real-time data analytics.

4. **Healthcare:** Supercomputers are used for medical imaging analysis, drug discovery, patient data analytics, and genomics

research, improving patient care and treatment outcomes.

5. **Manufacturing and Engineering:** Supercomputing aids in optimizing manufacturing processes, materials development, and aerodynamic simulations for industries like aerospace and automotive.

6. **Energy Sector:** The energy sector employs supercomputers for reservoir simulation, seismic data analysis, and energy grid optimization, enhancing energy exploration and distribution.

Challenges and Future Directions:

1. **Data Privacy and Security:** As data grows in size and importance, ensuring data privacy and cybersecurity in big data analytics is a growing concern.

2. **Energy Efficiency:** The power consumption of supercomputers can be significant, making energy-efficient designs and cooling systems a priority.

3. **Interoperability:** Ensuring compatibility and integration between different data sources and supercomputing systems is essential for seamless data analytics workflows.

4. **Scalability:** Supercomputing clusters must be scalable to accommodate growing data volumes and evolving analytics needs.

In conclusion, supercomputing is at the forefront of big data analytics, empowering organizations to extract valuable insights from massive datasets. From scientific breakthroughs to business intelligence and healthcare advancements, the synergy between supercomputing and big data analytics continues to drive innovation and address complex challenges across diverse domains. As data continues to proliferate, the role of supercomputing in shaping our data-driven future is bound to expand, enabling deeper insights and more informed decision-making.

D. AI and HPC Synergy: Advancing Science and Industry

The convergence of Artificial Intelligence (AI) and High-Performance Computing (HPC) represents a dynamic partnership that is revolutionizing science, industry, and technology across the globe. In this chapter, we'll delve into the symbiotic relationship between AI and HPC, uncovering how their combined powers are driving innovation, enabling groundbreaking research, and transforming industries.

The Symbiotic Relationship:

1. **AI's Appetite for Compute:** AI, particularly deep learning, demands immense computational resources for tasks like training complex neural networks on vast datasets. HPC

systems provide the computational horsepower required to accelerate AI model development and training.

2. **AI Enhancing HPC:** AI techniques, such as machine learning and data analytics, are integral to HPC workflows. AI helps in data preprocessing, optimization, anomaly detection, and decision-making, augmenting the capabilities of HPC simulations and scientific computing.

Applications of AI and HPC Synergy:

1. **Scientific Discovery:** In scientific research, AI and HPC collaborate to analyze complex datasets from genomics, particle physics, and climate modeling. This synergy accelerates discoveries, such as identifying new particles in colliders or predicting climate patterns.

2. **Drug Discovery:** AI-driven drug discovery involves screening vast chemical libraries. HPC facilitates the simulation of drug interactions, significantly reducing the time and cost of developing pharmaceuticals.

3. **Healthcare:** The synergy of AI and HPC aids in medical imaging analysis, disease diagnosis, and genomics research, advancing personalized medicine and improving patient care.

4. **Autonomous Systems:** In autonomous vehicles, drones, and robotics, AI processes sensory data in real-time, while HPC

ensures rapid decision-making and control, enhancing safety and performance.

5. **Financial Services:** AI-driven algorithms for high-frequency trading, risk assessment, and fraud detection leverage HPC's speed and parallel processing capabilities.

6. **Natural Language Processing (NLP):** HPC clusters power large-scale NLP tasks, including language translation, sentiment analysis, and chatbots, improving human-computer interactions.

Technological Advancements:

1. **Parallelism:** HPC's parallel processing capabilities are harnessed for training massive neural networks simultaneously, reducing training times from weeks to hours.

2. **Specialized Hardware:** Graphics Processing Units (GPUs) and Tensor Processing Units (TPUs) accelerate AI workloads within HPC systems, boosting performance.

3. **In-Memory Computing:** AI algorithms benefit from in-memory computing, where data resides in RAM, reducing latency and improving real-time AI inference.

4. **Big Data Processing:** HPC clusters handle the immense data volumes generated by AI applications, ensuring data storage, retrieval, and analysis at scale.

Challenges and Future Directions:

1. **Energy Efficiency:** As AI and HPC tasks become more demanding, energy-efficient designs and cooling solutions are essential to control power consumption.

2. **Data Management:** Managing and curating vast datasets for AI and HPC is a significant challenge, requiring scalable storage solutions.

3. **Interoperability:** Ensuring seamless integration of AI and HPC components, software, and tools is critical for efficient workflows.

4. **Ethical Considerations:** Ethical guidelines for AI and HPC, particularly in healthcare and autonomous systems, are essential to address biases, privacy, and accountability.

Real-World Impact:

1. **COVID-19 Research:** AI and HPC accelerated COVID-19 research, enabling protein folding simulations for vaccine development and predicting disease spread.

2. **Climate Modeling:** The synergy aids climate scientists in creating high-resolution climate models, offering valuable insights into climate change mitigation and adaptation.

3. **Astronomy:** AI and HPC are used to analyze astronomical

data, identifying exoplanets, tracking asteroids, and advancing our understanding of the universe.

4. **Materials Science:** AI-driven simulations and HPC optimize materials design for energy storage, lightweight composites, and more.

In conclusion, the symbiotic relationship between AI and HPC is reshaping our world, pushing the boundaries of scientific discovery and transforming industries. As technology continues to advance, this synergy will become even more integral to addressing complex challenges and unlocking the full potential of AI-driven insights and HPC's computational might. Together, AI and HPC form a powerful alliance driving innovation and propelling us into a future where science and technology know no bounds.

E. Challenges in Supercomputing for AI

Supercomputing plays a pivotal role in advancing artificial intelligence (AI), enabling the training of complex neural networks, simulations, and data-intensive computations critical for AI-driven applications. However, harnessing supercomputing for AI comes with several significant challenges that need to be addressed to fully unlock the potential of this powerful synergy.

1. Computational Demands:

AI, particularly deep learning, is computationally intensive. Training large neural networks with vast datasets demands massive computational power. Supercomputers must continuously evolve to meet these escalating computational demands.

2. Energy Efficiency:

As supercomputers grow in scale and complexity to meet AI demands, their power consumption increases substantially. Developing energy-efficient supercomputing solutions is critical to mitigate environmental impact and operational costs.

3. Memory and Storage Management:

AI models often require large memory capacities and high-speed storage systems for efficient data access. Balancing memory and storage with compute resources is a challenge, especially when handling big data.

4. Scalability:

AI applications must be scalable to leverage the full capabilities of supercomputing clusters. Ensuring that AI algorithms can efficiently utilize distributed computing resources is a complex task.

5. Data Movement Bottlenecks:

Transferring massive datasets between storage and processing units can become a bottleneck in AI workflows. Reducing data movement latency and optimizing data access are crucial.

6. Hardware Acceleration:

Graphics Processing Units (GPUs) and specialized AI accelerators like Tensor Processing Units (TPUs) are essential for efficient AI computations. Integrating and optimizing these hardware components in supercomputing architectures require expertise.

7. Algorithmic Optimization:

Developing AI algorithms that can fully exploit the parallel processing capabilities of supercomputers is a non-trivial challenge. Efficiently parallelizing AI workloads and minimizing communication overhead are ongoing research areas.

8. Software Complexity:

Managing the software stack for AI on supercomputers involves coordinating various libraries, frameworks, and tools. Ensuring compatibility, stability, and performance across this complex ecosystem is a significant challenge.

9. Interdisciplinary Collaboration:

Supercomputing experts and AI researchers must collaborate closely to bridge the gap between hardware and software. Effective interdisciplinary collaboration is essential to harness the full potential of supercomputing for AI.

10. Ethical Considerations:

AI-driven research, particularly in fields like healthcare and autonomous systems, raises ethical concerns regarding privacy, bias, and accountability. Addressing these ethical challenges is crucial for responsible AI use on supercomputing platforms.

11. Cost Constraints:

Building and maintaining supercomputers capable of supporting AI workloads is costly. Ensuring accessibility and affordability for researchers and organizations is an ongoing challenge.

12. Security Concerns:

Supercomputing environments must be secured to protect sensitive AI models and datasets from cyber threats. Ensuring robust cybersecurity in AI research is paramount.

13. Data Privacy:

Supercomputers often handle sensitive and proprietary data.

Safeguarding data privacy and ensuring compliance with data protection regulations is a significant challenge.

14. AI Model Interpretability:

Interpreting complex AI models trained on supercomputers is a challenge. Understanding and explaining AI decisions, especially in critical applications like healthcare, is essential.

15. Algorithm Bias:

AI models can inherit biases present in training data. Detecting and mitigating bias in AI algorithms used on supercomputing platforms is an ethical and technical challenge.

Addressing these challenges requires ongoing research, collaboration between AI and supercomputing experts, hardware and software advancements, and a commitment to ethical and sustainable AI practices. Overcoming these obstacles will pave the way for more powerful and responsible AI applications powered by supercomputing technologies.

CHAPTER 8

Supercomputing Challenges and Innovations

At the intersection of computational prowess and the thirst for knowledge lies the realm of supercomputing. This chapter embarks on a journey through the challenges and innovations that define this cutting-edge field. Supercomputers, the titans of computation, are tasked with solving the most intricate problems of our time. Yet, as they venture into the uncharted territories of science, industry, and technology, they are confronted by a myriad of challenges.

From the ceaseless quest for energy efficiency and the management of colossal datasets to the complexities of hardware and software optimization, supercomputing stands at the forefront of technological evolution. But, as challenges arise, so too do innovations emerge, pushing the boundaries of what is computationally possible.

This chapter is a testament to the relentless spirit of innovation that fuels supercomputing. It unveils the challenges that demand ingenious solutions and the innovations that define the future of computational capabilities. Supercomputing is not merely a tool; it's a testament to human ingenuity, where challenges are but stepping stones to greater heights of knowledge and achievement.

A. Big Data Challenges in Supercomputing

Supercomputing, with its immense processing power and parallel computing capabilities, is ideally suited to handle the deluge of data generated in today's data-driven world. However, harnessing the potential of big data in supercomputing comes with its own set of challenges, from managing data volume to ensuring data quality and optimizing data movement. This chapter explores the multifaceted challenges posed by big data in the context of supercomputing and the innovative solutions being developed to address them.

1. Data Volume and Velocity:

The sheer volume of data generated daily is staggering, and supercomputers must contend with the torrent of data pouring in from various sources. High-velocity data streams, such as sensor data, social media feeds, and scientific instruments, challenge supercomputing systems to process and analyze data in near real-time.

2. Data Storage and Retrieval:

Storing and retrieving vast amounts of data efficiently is a significant challenge. Supercomputers require high-capacity storage systems capable of handling rapid read and write operations to prevent data bottlenecks.

3. Data Quality and Cleanup:

Big data is often characterized by noise, missing values, and inconsistencies. Ensuring data quality is essential for meaningful analysis and results. Supercomputing systems must incorporate data preprocessing and cleaning steps as part of their workflows.

4. Data Integration:

In many cases, big data comes from diverse sources and in various formats. Integrating and harmonizing this heterogeneous data to derive insights can be complex, requiring advanced data integration techniques.

5. Data Security and Privacy:

Big data often includes sensitive or confidential information, making data security and privacy a paramount concern. Supercomputing systems must implement robust security measures to protect data from breaches or unauthorized access.

6. Scalability:

Big data applications must be scalable to leverage the full capabilities of supercomputing clusters. Ensuring that algorithms and software can efficiently utilize distributed computing resources is a complex task.

7. Data Movement Bottlenecks:

Transferring massive datasets between storage and processing units can become a bottleneck in big data workflows. Reducing data movement latency and optimizing data access are crucial.

8. Energy Efficiency:

As the processing of big data requires significant computational power and storage, energy efficiency becomes an important consideration to reduce both operational costs and environmental impact.

9. Data Governance and Compliance:

Ensuring data governance and compliance with regulations such as GDPR, HIPAA, or industry-specific standards is a challenge, particularly when handling sensitive data on supercomputing platforms.

10. Algorithm Selection and Optimization:

Selecting the right algorithms and optimizing them for specific big data tasks is essential. Supercomputing environments should support a range of algorithms and tools for efficient data analysis.

11. Real-Time Analytics:

For applications requiring real-time insights, supercomputers must process and analyze data streams without delays, necessitating the development of real-time analytics frameworks.

Innovations to Address Big Data Challenges:

1. **High-Performance Storage:** Innovations in high-capacity, high-speed storage systems, such as parallel file systems and distributed storage architectures, enhance data storage and retrieval efficiency.

2. **In-Memory Computing:** Supercomputers equipped with large memory capacities enable in-memory processing, reducing data access latency for big data analytics.

3. **Distributed Computing:** The adoption of distributed computing frameworks like Hadoop and Spark allows for parallel processing of big data across supercomputing clusters.

4. **Data Processing Pipelines:** Designing efficient data processing pipelines that include data cleaning, transformation, and analysis stages streamlines big data workflows.

5. **Data Stream Processing:** Real-time analytics frameworks like Apache Kafka and Apache Flink enable the processing of high-velocity data streams.

6. **Security Measures:** Advanced encryption, access controls, and authentication mechanisms bolster data security in supercomputing environments.

7. **Scalable Architectures:** Supercomputing architectures are continuously evolving to accommodate growing data volumes and enable efficient parallel processing.

8. **Energy-Efficient Supercomputing:** Innovations in cooling technologies, power management, and hardware design contribute to more energy-efficient supercomputing systems.

In conclusion, big data presents formidable challenges in the realm of supercomputing, but these challenges also drive innovation. As data continues to grow in volume and complexity, supercomputing systems will continue to evolve to meet the demands of data-driven research, industry, and innovation. The synergy between supercomputing and big data is a testament to human ingenuity, pushing the boundaries of what is computationally possible in the age of information.

B. Exascale Computing and Beyond: Pioneering the Frontier of Computational Power

In the relentless pursuit of ever-increasing computational capabilities, exascale computing represents a monumental milestone. But it's not the endpoint; it's a stepping stone to what lies beyond. This chapter ventures into the realm of exascale computing, delving into its significance, the challenges it poses, and the exciting innovations and possibilities that await as we push the boundaries of computational power even further.

Understanding Exascale Computing:

1. **What is Exascale Computing?** - Exascale computing refers to the ability of a supercomputer to perform a quintillion (10^18) calculations per second (exaFLOPS). It's a level of computational speed that was once considered science fiction but is now becoming a reality.

2. **Significance of Exascale Computing** - Exascale computing has the potential to revolutionize various fields, from scientific research and climate modeling to drug discovery, materials science, and artificial intelligence. It enables the simulation of more complex and detailed models, leading to groundbreaking discoveries.

Challenges on the Path to Exascale:

1. **Power Consumption:** Achieving exascale speeds comes with an enormous power consumption challenge. Supercomputers at this scale require massive amounts of energy, making energy efficiency a top priority.

2. **Hardware Reliability:** As the number of components in supercomputers grows, so does the likelihood of hardware failures. Ensuring reliability in exascale systems is a complex task.

3. **Data Movement:** Moving data efficiently between memory and processors in exascale systems is a significant challenge, as data movement can consume a substantial portion of the energy budget.

4. **Programming Complexity:** Developing software that can fully exploit exascale systems' parallelism and heterogeneity is challenging. Simplifying programming models while maintaining performance is crucial.

5. **Resilience:** Exascale systems must be resilient to hardware and software faults to ensure continuous operation. This requires advanced fault detection and recovery mechanisms.

Innovations in Exascale Computing:

1. **Advanced Architectures:** Exascale systems often adopt novel architectures, such as accelerators (e.g., GPUs) and custom processors, to improve computational efficiency.

2. **Energy-Efficient Designs:** Innovations in cooling solutions, power management, and energy-efficient components aim to mitigate the power consumption challenge.

3. **High-Bandwidth Memory:** High-bandwidth memory technologies reduce data movement bottlenecks by placing more data closer to the processing units.

4. **Parallelism and Scalability:** Exascale computing embraces extreme parallelism and scalability to distribute workloads efficiently across thousands or even millions of cores.

5. **Co-Design:** A co-design approach involves collaboration between hardware and software developers, optimizing both aspects for maximum performance.

Beyond Exascale:

1. **Zettascale Computing (10^21 FLOPS):** While exascale is groundbreaking, the computing world has its sights set on zettascale computing, a thousand times more powerful. This could enable even more detailed simulations, AI advancements, and scientific breakthroughs.

2. **Quantum Computing:** Quantum computing represents a paradigm shift, offering the potential for exponential computational power compared to classical computers. It holds promise for solving problems currently beyond the reach of classical supercomputers.

3. **Neuromorphic Computing:** Inspired by the human brain, neuromorphic computing aims to build computers that mimic

neural networks, potentially enabling highly efficient and brain-like processing for AI applications.

4. **Bio-Computing:** Bio-computing explores the use of biological materials and processes to perform computations, offering a radically different approach to computation.

Applications and Implications:

1. **Scientific Discovery:** Exascale and beyond computing will facilitate more accurate climate modeling, fundamental physics research, and drug discovery, leading to scientific breakthroughs.

2. **AI Advancements:** These computing capabilities will supercharge AI research, enabling faster training of massive neural networks and driving innovations in natural language processing, computer vision, and more.

3. **Materials Science:** Advanced simulations will accelerate materials discovery, leading to developments in materials for energy storage, lightweight composites, and more.

4. **Healthcare:** Drug discovery, genomics, and personalized medicine will benefit from the computational power to analyze vast datasets rapidly.

In conclusion, exascale computing marks a remarkable achievement in the history of technology, yet it is only a stepping stone to even greater computational capabilities. The challenges it presents inspire innovation, and the possibilities it unlocks hold the potential to transform our understanding of the universe, solve complex problems, and reshape industries. The journey to harnessing the full potential of exascale and beyond computing is a testament to human ingenuity and the unending pursuit of knowledge and discovery.

C. Supercomputing for Quantum Simulations: Bridging the Quantum Divide

Quantum simulations represent a remarkable intersection of two cutting-edge fields: quantum computing and supercomputing. While quantum computers have the potential to revolutionize computation by solving problems that are intractable for classical computers, they are still in their infancy. Supercomputing, on the other hand, is here and now, offering computational resources and expertise to simulate and understand quantum systems that are currently beyond the reach of quantum hardware. In this chapter, we'll delve into the significance, challenges, and innovations surrounding supercomputing for quantum simulations.

Understanding Quantum Simulations:

1. **Quantum Systems:** Quantum simulations aim to model and understand the behavior of quantum systems, which exhibit phenomena that classical computers struggle to simulate

accurately.

2. **Quantum Divide:** Quantum computers, while promising, are limited in scale and capability due to technical challenges. This creates a "quantum divide" where quantum simulations on classical supercomputers play a crucial role.

Significance of Supercomputing for Quantum Simulations:

1. **Complementing Quantum Hardware:** Quantum simulations on supercomputers complement quantum hardware by enabling the study of larger and more complex quantum systems that quantum computers cannot handle yet.

2. **Fundamental Research:** Quantum simulations provide insights into fundamental quantum physics, condensed matter physics, and quantum chemistry, advancing our understanding of the quantum world.

3. **Materials Science:** Simulating quantum materials allows for the discovery of new materials with unique properties, with applications in electronics, energy storage, and more.

Challenges in Supercomputing for Quantum Simulations:

1. **Exponential Complexity:** Quantum systems exhibit exponential complexity as the number of quantum particles increases. Simulating large quantum systems demands immense computational resources.

2. **Noise and Error Mitigation:** Quantum hardware introduces noise and errors, which must be accounted for in quantum simulations to produce reliable results.

3. **Quantum State Reconstruction:** Extracting accurate information about quantum states from noisy measurements is challenging and requires advanced techniques.

4. **Resource Allocation:** Ensuring that supercomputing resources are allocated efficiently for quantum simulations, considering the high demand for these resources, is a logistical challenge.

Innovations in Supercomputing for Quantum Simulations:

1. **Quantum-Classical Hybrid Algorithms:** Hybrid algorithms combine quantum and classical computing resources to perform more efficient quantum simulations.

2. **Error Correction Techniques:** Developing error correction codes and techniques to mitigate errors in quantum simulations.

3. **Quantum Approximate Optimization Algorithms (QAOA):** QAOA algorithms leverage quantum-inspired techniques for solving optimization problems, a crucial application in quantum simulations.

4. **Parallelization:** Utilizing the parallel processing capabilities

of supercomputers to distribute quantum simulations across multiple nodes efficiently.

Applications and Implications:

1. **Quantum Materials:** Quantum simulations aid in the discovery and characterization of novel materials with unique quantum properties.

2. **Quantum Chemistry:** Understanding molecular interactions at a quantum level has implications for drug discovery, catalysis, and materials science.

3. **Quantum Information Processing:** Quantum simulations are essential for advancing quantum algorithms and quantum error correction.

4. **Fundamental Physics:** Simulating complex quantum systems provides insights into fundamental physics questions, such as the behavior of matter under extreme conditions.

In conclusion, supercomputing for quantum simulations represents a bridge between the promise of quantum computing and the practical realities of today's computational capabilities. It enables us to explore the quantum realm, unlock new scientific insights, and potentially discover transformative technologies. As both quantum and classical computing continue to advance, the synergy between supercomputing and quantum simulations holds the potential to reshape industries and deepen our understanding of the quantum world.

D. Challenges in Supercomputing Sustainability

Supercomputing, with its immense computational power, has contributed significantly to scientific advancements, technological innovations, and industry breakthroughs. However, the rapid growth of supercomputing facilities has raised concerns about their environmental impact and energy consumption. This chapter explores the sustainability challenges associated with supercomputing and the strategies and innovations being developed to address them.

1. Energy Consumption:

Supercomputers are notorious energy hogs. They consume vast amounts of electricity, leading to high operational costs and a significant carbon footprint. As supercomputers continue to grow in scale and complexity, finding energy-efficient solutions is paramount.

2. Cooling Requirements:

Maintaining the optimal operating temperature of supercomputers is essential. Cooling systems can consume as much energy as the computing components themselves. Efficient cooling methods are crucial to reduce energy consumption.

3. Carbon Emissions:

The carbon emissions associated with supercomputing facilities contribute to climate change. Addressing these emissions is not only an environmental imperative but also a social responsibility.

4. Environmental Impact:

Supercomputing facilities often require large physical footprints, impacting local ecosystems and resources. Sustainable site selection and building practices are essential to mitigate environmental damage.

5. Electronic Waste:

The rapid turnover of supercomputing hardware generates electronic waste. Disposing of outdated components responsibly and recycling materials are sustainability challenges.

6. Scalability and Efficiency:

As supercomputers scale up in terms of the number of processors and components, ensuring that they remain energy-efficient becomes increasingly challenging.

7. Sustainable Hardware Design:

Developing energy-efficient processors, memory modules, and storage devices is crucial. Sustainable hardware design minimizes power consumption without compromising performance.

8. Renewable Energy Integration:

Harnessing renewable energy sources, such as solar and wind power, for supercomputing facilities can significantly reduce their carbon footprint. However, integrating renewables into existing infrastructures can be complex.

9. Energy Storage:

Efficient energy storage solutions, such as advanced batteries or supercapacitors, can help manage fluctuating energy demands in supercomputing facilities.

10. Energy-Aware Software:

Developing energy-aware software that optimizes code execution while minimizing power consumption is a challenge. Software must be designed to take advantage of hardware-level optimizations.

11. Resource Management:

Effective resource management, including dynamic voltage and frequency scaling (DVFS), is essential to match computing resources with workload demands and reduce energy waste.

12. Green Data Centers:

Designing and constructing green data centers that prioritize sustainability features like passive cooling, efficient power distribution, and energy-efficient lighting.

13. Training and Education:

Raising awareness about the importance of sustainability in supercomputing and providing training for data center personnel and researchers on energy-efficient practices.

Innovations for Sustainable Supercomputing:

1. **Liquid Cooling:** Immersion cooling and liquid-cooled systems are emerging as more energy-efficient alternatives to traditional air cooling.

2. **Advanced Power Management:** Techniques like power capping and dynamic power allocation help optimize energy usage in real-time.

3. **Green Procurement Policies:** Organizations are adopting green procurement policies to prioritize energy-efficient and sustainable hardware.

4. **Energy Monitoring and Reporting:** Advanced energy monitoring tools provide real-time insights into energy

consumption, helping organizations identify areas for improvement.

5. **Renewable Energy Integration:** Supercomputing centers are increasingly adopting renewable energy sources and power purchase agreements (PPAs) to reduce their carbon footprint.

6. **Waste Reduction Strategies:** Implementing strategies to reduce electronic waste, including recycling and repurposing components, extends the lifecycle of hardware.

7. **Collaborative Research:** International collaborations on sustainable supercomputing research promote the exchange of best practices and innovations.

Addressing sustainability challenges in supercomputing requires a multi-faceted approach that encompasses hardware and software optimization, energy-efficient data center design, and a commitment to reducing environmental impact. As supercomputing facilities continue to push the boundaries of computational capabilities, ensuring their sustainability is not just an environmental goal but also essential for long-term operational viability and responsible scientific advancement.

E. International Collaboration in Supercomputing: Advancing Together

Supercomputing is a global endeavor that transcends borders, languages, and cultures. In an increasingly interconnected world, international collaboration has become a cornerstone of progress in supercomputing. This chapter explores the significance, benefits, challenges, and notable examples of international collaboration in the realm of supercomputing.

Understanding International Collaboration in Supercomputing:

1. **Shared Goals:** International collaboration in supercomputing brings together researchers, scientists, and engineers from different countries and organizations to achieve common goals. These goals often revolve around advancing scientific research, solving complex problems, and driving technological innovation.

2. **Resource Sharing:** Collaborative efforts often involve sharing supercomputing resources, expertise, and data. This sharing amplifies the capabilities of individual institutions and accelerates progress.

Significance of International Collaboration:

1. **Pooling Resources:** Supercomputing centers worldwide vary in their computing power, specialization, and research strengths. Collaboration allows access to a broader spectrum of resources, from computing clusters to specialized hardware.

2. **Knowledge Exchange:** Collaboration fosters the exchange of knowledge, best practices, and expertise among researchers and institutions. It enhances the collective understanding of supercomputing technologies and their applications.

3. **Accelerating Research:** International collaboration accelerates research by bringing together diverse perspectives, facilitating data sharing, and enabling collaborative problem-solving. This can lead to breakthroughs in various fields.

Challenges in International Collaboration:

1. **Policy and Regulations:** Differences in national policies, export controls, and intellectual property laws can pose challenges to international data and resource sharing.

2. **Language and Communication:** Effective collaboration requires clear communication, and language barriers can hinder the exchange of ideas and information.

3. **Data Privacy and Security:** Ensuring data privacy and security in cross-border collaborations is a complex issue, especially when sensitive or proprietary data is involved.

4. **Cultural Differences:** Collaborators from different cultural backgrounds may have varying approaches to problem-solving and decision-making, requiring effective cross-cultural communication and understanding.

Notable Examples of International Collaboration:

1. **European High-Performance Computing Initiative (EuroHPC):** EuroHPC is a European Union initiative that aims to create a world-class supercomputing ecosystem. It involves collaboration among EU member states and associated countries.

2. **International Research Organizations:** Organizations like CERN (European Organization for Nuclear Research) and ITER (International Thermonuclear Experimental Reactor) rely on international collaboration and supercomputing to conduct cutting-edge research in particle physics and nuclear fusion.

3. **Joint Research Projects:** Researchers from different countries often collaborate on joint research projects that require significant computational resources. For example, climate modeling projects involve scientists from around the world working together to understand climate change.

4. **Open Source Software Development:** The development of open-source software for supercomputing, such as the Message Passing Interface (MPI), often involves contributions from researchers and developers worldwide.

Benefits of International Collaboration:

1. **Access to Leading Technologies:** Collaborators gain access to cutting-edge supercomputing technologies and infrastructure that may not be available domestically.

2. **Leveraging Diverse Expertise:** International collaboration brings together experts from various domains, enhancing problem-solving and innovation.

3. **Cost Sharing:** Sharing the financial burden of supercomputing infrastructure and research projects is cost-effective and efficient.

4. **Global Impact:** Collaborative research projects have a broader and more significant impact, addressing global challenges that transcend national boundaries.

5. **Cultural Enrichment:** Collaboration fosters cultural exchange and mutual understanding, enriching the global scientific community.

In conclusion, international collaboration in supercomputing is not merely a choice but a necessity in today's interconnected world. It amplifies the capabilities of individual researchers and institutions, accelerates scientific discovery, and addresses complex global challenges. By bridging geographic and cultural divides, international collaboration in supercomputing exemplifies the shared pursuit of knowledge and the power of collective efforts to advance science and technology for the betterment of humanity.

CHAPTER 9

Supercomputing Case Studies and Success Stories

In the world of supercomputing, where computational power knows no bounds, stories of innovation, discovery, and transformation are written every day. This chapter invites you to delve into the real-world implementations, challenges overcome, and innovations that have reshaped industries and pushed the boundaries of human knowledge. From unraveling the mysteries of the cosmos to accelerating breakthroughs in healthcare and industry-specific applications, the case studies and success stories within these pages showcase the extraordinary power and potential of supercomputing. These narratives are a testament to human ingenuity and the remarkable achievements made possible when science, technology, and ambition unite on a global scale. Join us on this journey through the frontiers of computational excellence, where each success story is a stepping stone toward a more informed, innovative, and interconnected world.

A. Real-world Implementations of Supercomputing: Transforming Industries and Advancing Knowledge

Supercomputing, once a niche domain, has permeated virtually every facet of modern life. Its enormous computational power and ability to process vast datasets have revolutionized industries and propelled scientific research to new heights. In this chapter, we explore real-world implementations of supercomputing, showcasing how these high-performance machines have transformed various sectors, from scientific research and healthcare to manufacturing and finance.

Scientific Research:

1. **Astrophysics and Cosmology:** Supercomputers are instrumental in simulating complex celestial phenomena, aiding our understanding of the universe's origins and evolution. They model black holes, galaxy formation, and cosmic microwave background radiation.

2. **Climate Modeling:** Climate scientists use supercomputers to run intricate climate models, predicting climate change patterns, extreme weather events, and the impacts of greenhouse gas emissions.

3. **Particle Physics:** Facilities like CERN rely on supercomputing for data analysis and simulations. It played a crucial role in discovering the Higgs boson.

4. **Drug Discovery:** Pharmaceutical companies use supercomputing to screen and design new drug candidates, significantly accelerating the drug discovery process.

5. **Materials Science:** Supercomputers simulate materials at the atomic level, aiding in the development of advanced materials for industries like aerospace and electronics.

Healthcare:

1. **Genomics:** Supercomputing accelerates genomic research by analyzing massive DNA sequences, enabling personalized medicine and insights into genetic diseases.

2. **Drug Design:** Supercomputers simulate drug interactions with biomolecules, reducing the time and cost of drug development.

3. **Medical Imaging:** High-resolution medical imaging, such as MRI and CT scans, benefits from supercomputing's image processing capabilities, aiding diagnosis and treatment planning.

Manufacturing:

1. **Aerospace:** Aircraft and spacecraft design rely on supercomputing for simulations that optimize aerodynamics, reduce fuel consumption, and enhance safety.

2. **Automotive:** Supercomputing enables advanced simulations for crash testing, vehicle design, and fuel efficiency improvements.

3. **Energy:** Supercomputers model fluid dynamics and structural integrity in power plants, aiding in energy production and safety.

Finance:

1. **Risk Assessment:** Supercomputing performs complex financial modeling and risk assessments, crucial for investment decisions and managing portfolios.

2. **Algorithmic Trading:** High-frequency trading firms use supercomputing for real-time analysis and rapid execution of trading strategies.

Entertainment:

1. **Film and Animation:** Supercomputers render complex CGI scenes, enhancing the realism and visual effects of movies, video games, and animations.

National Security:

1. **Cybersecurity:** Supercomputers bolster cybersecurity efforts by analyzing network traffic patterns and identifying vulnerabilities.

2. **Nuclear Simulation:** Nuclear weapons simulations, used for testing and disarmament purposes, rely on supercomputing to model nuclear reactions and their effects.

Environmental Sciences:

1. **Ecological Modeling:** Supercomputing aids in ecological modeling, assessing environmental impacts, and developing conservation strategies.

2. **Natural Disaster Prediction:** Advanced simulations help predict natural disasters like earthquakes, tsunamis, and hurricanes, improving preparedness and response.

Challenges in Real-world Implementations:

1. **Data Management:** Handling massive datasets generated by supercomputing simulations is a logistical challenge.

2. **Energy Consumption:** The energy requirements of supercomputing facilities pose environmental and operational challenges.

3. **Cost:** Building and maintaining supercomputing systems are expensive endeavors, often requiring substantial investments.

Innovations and Future Directions:

1. **Exascale Computing:** The race toward exascale computing promises even greater computational power, unlocking new

possibilities in research and industry.

2. **Quantum Supercomputing:** Quantum computing, when mature, may revolutionize computing and further expand the horizons of what's possible.

3. **AI Integration:** Combining supercomputing with artificial intelligence enhances data analysis, optimization, and decision-making.

In conclusion, real-world implementations of supercomputing are as diverse as the challenges they address and the innovations they enable. From scientific breakthroughs to industrial advancements and beyond, supercomputing continues to reshape our world and drive progress across a multitude of disciplines. As we stand at the brink of exascale and quantum computing eras, the future holds the promise of even greater discoveries and innovations driven by the unparalleled power of supercomputing.

B. Industry-specific Case Studies: Harnessing Supercomputing for Innovation and Efficiency

Supercomputing's immense computational power and data processing capabilities have revolutionized industries across the spectrum. In this chapter, we delve into industry-specific case studies that exemplify the transformative impact of supercomputing, from optimizing manufacturing processes to enhancing financial modeling and everything in between.

Manufacturing:

1. **Aerospace Advancements:** Aircraft design and simulation have seen a remarkable transformation. Firms like Boeing use supercomputing for aerodynamic modeling, structural analysis, and crash simulations, reducing development time and improving fuel efficiency. Supercomputing helps design more fuel-efficient aircraft while ensuring passenger safety.

2. **Automotive Engineering:** Leading car manufacturers like BMW leverage supercomputing for crash tests, aerodynamics, and engine design. Simulations enable them to assess vehicle safety, reduce fuel consumption, and develop electric and autonomous vehicles.

3. **Energy Efficiency in Oil and Gas:** The energy industry uses supercomputers for reservoir modeling, seismic imaging, and drilling optimization. Companies like Chevron and BP rely on these simulations to locate oil reserves, minimize environmental impact, and improve energy extraction.

Financial Services:

1. **Risk Assessment:** Investment banks employ supercomputing to assess and manage financial risks. Case studies from firms

like JPMorgan Chase and Goldman Sachs showcase how supercomputers analyze market data in real-time, model complex financial instruments, and make rapid trading decisions.

2. **Fraud Detection:** Credit card companies like Visa and Mastercard use supercomputing for fraud detection. Machine learning algorithms analyze vast transaction datasets to identify unusual patterns and prevent fraudulent activities.

Healthcare and Pharmaceuticals:

1. **Drug Discovery:** Pharmaceutical giants like Pfizer and Novartis rely on supercomputing to accelerate drug discovery. Molecular simulations help in designing new drugs, understanding their interactions with biological molecules, and predicting potential side effects.

2. **Genomics Research:** Genomic research centers, such as the Broad Institute, use supercomputing to analyze massive genomic datasets. This accelerates advancements in personalized medicine, genetic disease understanding, and drug development.

Energy and Environment:

1. **Renewable Energy:** Renewable energy companies, like Vestas Wind Systems, employ supercomputing for wind farm

optimization. Simulations model wind patterns and turbine designs, maximizing energy production and reducing costs.

2. **Climate Modeling:** Climate research centers, including the UK Met Office and the National Center for Atmospheric Research (NCAR), use supercomputing for climate modeling. These models predict climate change patterns, extreme weather events, and their impacts on ecosystems and society.

Entertainment and Media:

1. **Film Production:** Hollywood studios like Pixar and Weta Digital rely on supercomputing for rendering complex CGI scenes in blockbuster movies. These simulations enhance visual effects and bring imagination to life on the big screen.

National Defense and Security:

1. **Nuclear Simulations:** National laboratories like Los Alamos National Laboratory and Sandia National Laboratories use supercomputing to simulate nuclear weapon behavior. These simulations aid in the assessment of nuclear stockpile reliability and disarmament efforts.

2. **Cybersecurity:** Government agencies and cybersecurity firms employ supercomputing to analyze network traffic, detect threats, and protect critical infrastructure from cyberattacks.

Challenges and Innovations:

1. **Data Management:** Managing the massive datasets generated by supercomputing simulations requires advanced storage solutions and data analytics tools.

2. **Energy Efficiency:** Supercomputing centers are investing in energy-efficient cooling and power management solutions to mitigate high energy consumption.

3. **Custom Hardware:** Customized processors and accelerators like GPUs are increasingly used to optimize supercomputing for specific workloads.

4. **Exascale Computing:** The race to exascale computing promises even greater computational power for solving industry-specific challenges.

These case studies demonstrate that supercomputing is not just a scientific endeavor but a driving force behind innovation and efficiency in diverse industries. As supercomputers continue to advance, their potential to revolutionize industry-specific processes and create groundbreaking solutions is boundless, contributing to the betterment of society and the global economy.

C. Challenges Faced and Overcome in Supercomputing

Supercomputing, while a powerful tool, is not without its share of challenges. These high-performance machines are at the forefront of technology and scientific discovery, but they also face obstacles that must be addressed to unleash their full potential. In this chapter, we examine some of the critical challenges faced by supercomputing and the ingenious solutions developed to conquer them.

1. Energy Consumption:

Challenge: Supercomputers are notorious energy consumers, with power-hungry processors and cooling systems. Operating them efficiently while minimizing their carbon footprint is a significant challenge.

Solution: To address this challenge, supercomputing centers are implementing energy-efficient cooling techniques, such as liquid cooling and warm water cooling. Advanced power management systems, including dynamic voltage and frequency scaling (DVFS), help optimize energy usage. Renewable energy sources, such as solar and wind power, are integrated into data centers to reduce their environmental impact.

2. Data Management:

Challenge: Supercomputers generate massive datasets, which can overwhelm storage and data management systems. Efficiently storing, accessing, and analyzing these datasets pose logistical challenges.

Solution: Supercomputing centers invest in high-performance storage solutions, including parallel file systems and distributed storage architectures. They also utilize data compression and deduplication techniques to reduce storage requirements. Data analytics tools are employed to process and gain insights from these vast datasets efficiently.

3. Scalability:

Challenge: As supercomputers scale up in terms of the number of processors and components, ensuring that they remain efficient and effective becomes increasingly challenging. Achieving strong scaling, where adding more resources results in proportionate performance improvements, is not always straightforward.

Solution: Researchers and engineers are developing parallel programming techniques that allow software to leverage the increasing number of processing cores effectively. Advanced algorithms and message-passing libraries like MPI enable parallel execution. Co-design, where hardware and software are developed together, ensures that supercomputers are optimized for specific workloads.

4. Hardware Reliability:

Challenge: Supercomputers consist of thousands of components, and hardware failures are inevitable. These failures can disrupt simulations and research projects.

Solution: Supercomputing centers implement redundancy and fault-tolerant mechanisms to mitigate hardware failures. Hardware diagnostics and monitoring tools constantly assess the health of components, enabling proactive maintenance. Virtualization and containerization technologies isolate software from hardware, improving reliability.

5. Programming Complexity:

Challenge: Writing software for supercomputers can be complex and requires expertise in parallel programming. The diverse architectures of supercomputers demand tailored software development.

Solution: Software development frameworks like OpenMP and CUDA simplify parallel programming. Training programs and resources are available to educate researchers and developers in the intricacies of supercomputing software development.

6. Data Security:

Challenge: Supercomputers handle sensitive research data, raising concerns about data security and protecting against cyberattacks.

Solution: Supercomputing centers implement robust cybersecurity measures, including firewalls, intrusion detection systems, and encryption. They also educate users about best practices for data security.

7. Cost:

Challenge: Building and maintaining supercomputers is expensive. Funding and operational costs can be prohibitive for some organizations.

Solution: Governments and research institutions often collaborate to pool resources and share the financial burden. Cloud-based supercomputing services also provide cost-effective access to high-performance computing resources.

8. Software Compatibility:

Challenge: Software developed for one supercomputer may not run efficiently on another due to differences in architectures and configurations.

Solution: Standardization efforts and compatibility layers aim to make software more portable across different supercomputing platforms. Containerization technologies like Docker enable applications to run consistently across diverse environments.

9. Exascale Computing:

Challenge: Achieving exascale computing, where supercomputers can perform a billion billion calculations per second, poses monumental technical and infrastructure challenges.

Solution: Researchers are developing novel hardware architectures, energy-efficient components, and software optimizations to realize exascale computing. International collaborations are critical to pool expertise and resources in this ambitious endeavor.

In conclusion, supercomputing's challenges are met with resilience and innovation. Researchers, engineers, and organizations collaborate to push the boundaries of what is possible, addressing energy consumption, data management, scalability, and other hurdles. As supercomputers continue to evolve, their potential to transform industries and advance scientific knowledge remains as promising as ever, and the lessons learned from overcoming these challenges will continue to drive progress in the field.

D. Innovations and Lessons Learned in Supercomputing

Supercomputing is a field defined by relentless innovation,

where lessons learned from the past inspire breakthroughs that drive the future. In this chapter, we examine some of the most remarkable innovations that have shaped supercomputing and the invaluable lessons that continue to guide its evolution.

Innovations:

1. Parallel Processing:

Innovation: The concept of parallel processing, where multiple processors work simultaneously on different parts of a problem, revolutionized supercomputing. Innovations like Message Passing Interface (MPI) and OpenMP paved the way for efficient parallel programming.

Impact: Parallel processing transformed supercomputing from a single-processor model to massively parallel systems. It exponentially increased computational power and enabled simulations of unprecedented complexity.

2. Moore's Law:

Innovation: Gordon Moore's observation that the number of transistors on a microchip doubles approximately every two years laid the foundation for the relentless pace of hardware innovation in supercomputing.

Impact: Moore's Law has driven the consistent increase in processor speed, memory capacity, and overall computing power.

It remains a guiding principle for hardware development.

3. CUDA and GPU Computing:

Innovation: NVIDIA's CUDA (Compute Unified Device Architecture) introduced the concept of general-purpose GPU computing, allowing GPUs to be used not only for graphics but also for scientific simulations and data processing.

Impact: CUDA and GPU computing significantly accelerated scientific research and made supercomputing more accessible to researchers across various domains.

4. Big Data Analytics:

Innovation: The advent of supercomputing-based big data analytics tools and frameworks, such as Hadoop and Spark, revolutionized data processing and analysis capabilities.

Impact: Big data analytics on supercomputers enabled researchers and organizations to extract valuable insights from vast datasets, with applications in fields ranging from genomics to finance.

5. Quantum Computing:

Innovation: Quantum computing, though still in its infancy, holds the promise of revolutionizing computing by harnessing the principles of quantum mechanics for unprecedented computational power.

Impact: Quantum computing has the potential to solve complex problems that are currently beyond the reach of classical supercomputers, such as simulating quantum systems and cracking encryption codes.

Lessons Learned:

1. Energy Efficiency:

Lesson Learned: The importance of energy-efficient supercomputing cannot be overstated. High energy consumption not only impacts operational costs but also has environmental implications.

Application: Supercomputing centers invest in energy-efficient cooling solutions, employ power management techniques, and explore renewable energy sources to reduce their carbon footprint.

2. Software Optimization:

Lesson Learned: Developing efficient software for supercomputers is as crucial as building powerful hardware. Software must be optimized to take full advantage of the hardware's capabilities.

Application: Parallel programming techniques, code

optimization, and software libraries continue to evolve to ensure that software can exploit the parallelism of supercomputing architectures.

3. Collaboration and Open Source:

Lesson Learned: Collaboration and open-source development foster innovation and the sharing of knowledge. Many supercomputing tools and libraries are open source, enabling a global community of researchers and developers to contribute.

Application: Open-source projects like Linux, MPI, and OpenMP have become essential components of supercomputing ecosystems, promoting collaboration and knowledge exchange.

4. Sustainability:

Lesson Learned: Supercomputing's growth must be sustainable, considering both economic and environmental factors.

Application: Sustainability initiatives include energy-efficient data centers, recycling of electronic waste, and international collaborations to maximize resource utilization.

5. Interdisciplinary Collaboration:

Lesson Learned: The most significant breakthroughs often occur at the intersection of different disciplines. Interdisciplinary collaboration sparks innovation.

Application: Cross-disciplinary research initiatives bring together experts from diverse fields, enabling the development of supercomputing solutions for complex, real-world problems.

In conclusion, supercomputing's innovations and lessons learned have shaped its evolution into a field that continues to push the boundaries of computational capability. Innovations in parallel processing, GPU computing, and quantum computing have revolutionized computing power, while lessons about energy efficiency, software optimization, collaboration, and sustainability guide its responsible growth. As supercomputers venture into the exascale and quantum computing eras, the enduring principles of innovation and adaptability remain at the heart of the field's progress, promising exciting possibilities for the future.

CHAPTER 10

Future Trends and Innovations in Supercomputing: Pioneering the Next Frontier

In the ever-evolving landscape of supercomputing, the horizon is painted with promises of greater computational power, novel architectures, and groundbreaking applications. This chapter embarks on a journey into the future of supercomputing, where innovation knows no bounds, and the boundaries of human knowledge are relentlessly pushed. Join us as we explore the emerging trends, transformative technologies, and visionary innovations that are poised to shape the supercomputing landscape for years to come. From the advent of exascale computing to the revolutionary potential of quantum supercomputers, this chapter offers a glimpse into a world where the computational limits are defined only by the extent of our imagination.

A. The Evolution of Supercomputing: From Humble Beginnings to Exascale Frontiers

The history of supercomputing is a testament to humanity's unceasing quest for computational power and its boundless curiosity to explore the frontiers of science and technology. In this chapter, we embark on a retrospective journey through the evolution of supercomputing, tracing its humble beginnings, major milestones, and the transformative innovations that have propelled it to the brink of the exascale era.

Humble Beginnings:

Supercomputing's roots can be traced back to the mid-20th century, a time when electronic computers were in their infancy. Early machines like the ENIAC (Electronic Numerical Integrator and Computer) were colossal, room-filling behemoths that performed calculations at speeds unimaginable by human standards. These early computers, while revolutionary, lacked the sophistication and computational power that define modern supercomputers.

The Emergence of Vector Supercomputers:

In the 1970s, the introduction of vector processing marked a significant leap in supercomputing capabilities. Vector supercomputers, exemplified by the Cray-1, pioneered the use of vector pipelines to perform mathematical operations rapidly. This innovation enabled scientists and engineers to simulate complex physical phenomena with greater accuracy and efficiency.

Parallel Processing Paradigm:

The 1980s brought a fundamental shift in supercomputing architecture with the advent of parallel processing. Instead of relying solely on single, high-speed processors, supercomputers began to incorporate multiple processors that worked in parallel. This paradigm shift allowed for the efficient execution of parallel algorithms, significantly enhancing computational performance. Machines like the Connection Machine and the Thinking Machines CM-5 exemplified this era of supercomputing.

Massively Parallel Processing (MPP) Systems:

The 1990s witnessed the rise of Massively Parallel Processing (MPP) systems, characterized by clusters of off-the-shelf processors interconnected to perform parallel computations. These machines, such as the Cray T3D and the IBM SP2, were more cost-effective and scalable than their predecessors. MPP systems found applications in diverse fields, from weather prediction and climate modeling to molecular dynamics simulations.

The High-Performance Computing (HPC) Revolution:

In the 21st century, supercomputing transcended its traditional role in scientific research and became a cornerstone of high-performance computing (HPC). The Blue Gene series by IBM, for instance, was designed to tackle grand challenges in biology, materials science, and astrophysics.

GPU Acceleration and Heterogeneous Computing:

A pivotal moment in supercomputing history came with the integration of Graphics Processing Units (GPUs) for general-purpose computing. NVIDIA's CUDA architecture and AMD's stream processing technology revolutionized supercomputing by harnessing the immense parallel processing power of GPUs. This approach not only significantly boosted computational performance but also broadened supercomputing's accessibility to a wider range of applications, including artificial intelligence and deep learning.

Exascale Computing on the Horizon:

As we venture into the 2020s and beyond, the supercomputing community stands at the precipice of exascale computing, where supercomputers will perform one quintillion (10^{18}) calculations per second. Exascale computing holds the promise of unraveling the mysteries of the universe, simulating complex biological systems, and addressing global challenges like climate change and energy sustainability.

Quantum Supercomputing:

Simultaneously, quantum computing has emerged as a disruptive force in the supercomputing landscape. Quantum supercomputers, while still in their infancy, have the potential to tackle problems that are practically unsolvable by classical supercomputers, including cryptography, optimization, and simulating quantum systems.

The Ever-Present Challenges:

Throughout its evolution, supercomputing has grappled with challenges such as energy consumption, data management, and software optimization. Innovations in cooling techniques, energy-efficient components, and parallel programming languages continue to address these issues.

In conclusion, the evolution of supercomputing is a testament to human ingenuity and the relentless pursuit of computational excellence. From humble beginnings to the exascale and quantum frontiers, supercomputers have transformed scientific research, industry, and society as a whole. As we stand on the cusp of unparalleled computational power, the future of supercomputing promises to be a thrilling journey into uncharted territory, where the boundaries of knowledge and discovery are defined only by the limits of our imagination.

B. Quantum Supercomputing and Quantum Advantage: A Paradigm Shift in Computing

Quantum computing is a technological marvel that stands poised to revolutionize the world of computation. While classical supercomputers have pushed the boundaries of what's possible, quantum supercomputing promises to shatter these boundaries by harnessing the principles of quantum mechanics. In this chapter, we explore quantum supercomputing and the elusive concept of quantum advantage, a paradigm shift that could reshape industries and solve problems previously deemed insurmountable.

Quantum Computing Fundamentals:

At the heart of quantum computing lies the quantum bit or qubit. Unlike classical bits, which can be either 0 or 1, qubits can exist in multiple states simultaneously, a phenomenon known as superposition. Additionally, qubits can be entangled, meaning the state of one qubit is intrinsically linked to the state of another, even if separated by vast distances. These properties allow quantum computers to perform certain calculations exponentially faster than classical computers.

Quantum Superposition and Entanglement:

1. **Superposition:** Qubits can represent a combination of 0 and 1 at the same time, allowing quantum computers to explore multiple solutions to a problem simultaneously. This provides exponential speedup for specific algorithms, such as Shor's algorithm for factoring large numbers and Grover's algorithm for searching unsorted databases.

2. **Entanglement:** Entanglement enables qubits to work together in ways that classical bits cannot. It enables quantum

computers to perform complex operations on large datasets efficiently.

Applications of Quantum Computing:

Quantum computing holds the potential to revolutionize various fields:

1. **Cryptography:** Quantum computers could break widely-used encryption methods, spurring the development of quantum-resistant encryption techniques.

2. **Optimization:** Quantum algorithms can solve complex optimization problems, such as portfolio optimization in finance and logistics planning, much faster than classical computers.

3. **Drug Discovery:** Simulating molecular interactions for drug discovery and materials science is a promising application.

4. **Machine Learning:** Quantum machine learning algorithms promise faster training and inference, opening new avenues for artificial intelligence.

Challenges in Quantum Computing:

While the potential of quantum computing is vast, there are significant challenges:

1. **Error Correction:** Quantum bits are highly susceptible to

errors due to their delicate quantum states. Developing robust error correction codes is essential for reliable quantum computing.

2. **Quantum Decoherence:** Qubits are sensitive to their environment, leading to decoherence, which disrupts quantum computations. Keeping qubits stable is a critical challenge.

3. **Hardware Development:** Building practical quantum processors that can scale to large numbers of qubits is an ongoing challenge for researchers and engineers.

Quantum Advantage:

The concept of quantum advantage refers to the point at which quantum computers outperform the most advanced classical supercomputers in solving specific problems. Achieving quantum advantage would mark a watershed moment in the field of computing, with profound implications for various industries.

Quantum Supremacy: A related term, quantum supremacy, denotes the point at which a quantum computer performs a calculation that is practically impossible for classical computers to replicate in a reasonable amount of time. In 2019, Google claimed to achieve quantum supremacy with their 53-qubit quantum processor, Sycamore, which solved a specialized problem faster than any classical computer could.

The Path Forward:

Quantum computing is still in its infancy, with many technical challenges to overcome. However, significant investments from governments and private companies are driving progress. Cloud-based quantum computing platforms are emerging, allowing researchers and developers to experiment with quantum algorithms and accelerate the development of quantum applications.

As quantum computers grow in scale and sophistication, the concept of quantum advantage will become increasingly relevant. It has the potential to disrupt industries, revolutionize cryptography, and unlock new realms of scientific discovery. While we are still on the journey toward quantum advantage, the destination promises to be a transformative moment in the history of computing, rivaling the impact of classical supercomputing in its ability to reshape the world as we know it.

C. Edge Supercomputing and IoT: Pioneering Computational Power at the Network's Edge

The convergence of Edge Supercomputing and the Internet of Things (IoT) represents a paradigm shift in computing, where computational power is pushed closer to the data source and the physical world. In this chapter, we explore the synergistic relationship between Edge Supercomputing and IoT, highlighting the transformative potential of this technological fusion.

Understanding Edge Supercomputing:

Edge Supercomputing, often referred to as "supercomputing at the edge," involves deploying high-performance computing resources, akin to those found in traditional supercomputers, at the network's edge or in close proximity to data sources. This strategic placement of computing power at the edge of the network, near IoT devices and sensors, enables real-time data processing, analysis, and decision-making.

Key Characteristics of Edge Supercomputing:

1. **Low Latency:** By reducing the distance that data needs to travel to reach a central data center or cloud, Edge Supercomputing minimizes network latency. This is crucial for applications that require instant responses, such as autonomous vehicles and industrial automation.

2. **Data Processing Onsite:** Edge Supercomputers process data locally, alleviating the burden on centralized data centers and reducing the volume of data that needs to be transmitted over the network. This is particularly advantageous for applications with limited bandwidth.

3. **Real-time Insights:** The proximity of Edge Supercomputing to IoT devices allows for real-time analysis of sensor data.

This capability is invaluable for applications like predictive maintenance in manufacturing and healthcare monitoring.

4. **Privacy and Security:** Data can be processed and analyzed at the edge, minimizing the need to transmit sensitive information to external servers, thereby enhancing data privacy and security.

IoT's Role in Edge Supercomputing:

The Internet of Things represents a vast ecosystem of interconnected sensors, devices, and systems that collect and exchange data. IoT devices generate an unprecedented volume of data, which, when combined with Edge Supercomputing, opens up new possibilities:

1. **Smart Cities:** IoT sensors in urban environments can monitor traffic, air quality, and public safety. Edge Supercomputing processes this data to optimize traffic flow, reduce pollution, and enhance security.

2. **Precision Agriculture:** In agriculture, IoT devices gather data on soil conditions, weather, and crop health. Edge Supercomputing analyzes this data to optimize irrigation, fertilization, and pest control, increasing crop yields and sustainability.

3. **Healthcare:** Wearable IoT devices continuously monitor vital

signs and transmit data to Edge Supercomputers, enabling early disease detection and personalized treatment recommendations.

4. **Manufacturing:** IoT sensors in manufacturing plants track equipment performance and detect anomalies. Edge Supercomputing ensures timely maintenance and reduces costly downtime.

Challenges and Considerations:

Despite its potential, Edge Supercomputing and IoT integration come with challenges:

1. **Scalability:** Deploying and managing Edge Supercomputing infrastructure at scale can be complex, especially in distributed IoT environments.

2. **Data Management:** Ensuring data integrity, security, and compliance at the edge is paramount. Edge Supercomputing solutions must include robust data management strategies.

3. **Resource Constraints:** Edge devices often have limited computational resources and power constraints. Optimizing algorithms and workloads for these environments is crucial.

4. **Interoperability:** Ensuring that IoT devices from various manufacturers can seamlessly connect to Edge Supercomputing resources requires standardized protocols

and interfaces.

The Future of Edge Supercomputing and IoT:

The future of Edge Supercomputing and IoT holds tremendous promise. As technology continues to advance, we can expect:

1. **Greater Autonomy:** Autonomous systems, from self-driving cars to smart factories, will rely heavily on Edge Supercomputing and IoT for real-time decision-making.

2. **Enhanced Data Analytics:** Advanced analytics, including machine learning and AI, will be integrated into Edge Supercomputing solutions, enabling deeper insights and predictive capabilities.

3. **5G Connectivity:** The rollout of 5G networks will further enable Edge Supercomputing, as high-speed, low-latency connections become more widespread.

4. **Expanding Use Cases:** New and innovative applications will emerge across industries, transforming the way we live and work.

In conclusion, the integration of Edge Supercomputing and IoT represents a dynamic shift in computing, bringing unprecedented computational power and real-time capabilities to the network's edge. This convergence promises to drive innovation, enhance efficiency, and improve our quality of life, setting the stage for a future where computing power is truly ubiquitous and transformative.:

D. Supercomputing for Healthcare and Drug Discovery: Transforming Medicine and Saving Lives

Supercomputing has emerged as a game-changer in the field of healthcare and drug discovery, offering computational capabilities that were once unimaginable. In this chapter, we delve into the profound impact of supercomputing in these domains, from accelerating drug development to personalized medicine and the simulation of complex biological systems.

1. Drug Discovery and Development:

1.1 Drug Discovery Process:

Drug discovery is a complex and resource-intensive process that involves the identification of potential drug candidates and their subsequent development. Supercomputing accelerates this process at multiple stages:

1.2 Drug Design and Molecular Modeling:

Supercomputers simulate molecular interactions at an atomic level, enabling researchers to design and test new drug compounds. Molecular dynamics simulations provide insights into how drugs interact with target proteins, leading to the optimization of drug candidates for efficacy and safety.

1.3 Virtual Screening and High-Throughput Screening:

Supercomputers facilitate virtual screening, where vast databases of chemical compounds are screened computationally to identify potential drug candidates. High-throughput screening is further accelerated through supercomputing, expediting the identification of lead compounds.

1.4 Drug-Drug Interactions and Side Effects:

Supercomputers analyze potential drug-drug interactions and predict side effects, improving drug safety profiles. This reduces the likelihood of adverse reactions during clinical trials and post-market surveillance.

2. Personalized Medicine:

Supercomputing enables the concept of personalized medicine, tailoring treatment plans to an individual's genetic makeup and specific disease characteristics. This approach maximizes treatment efficacy while minimizing side effects. Applications include:

2.1 Genomic Analysis:

Supercomputers analyze vast genomic datasets to identify

genetic markers associated with diseases, enabling precision medicine and targeted therapies.

2.2 Drug Response Prediction:

By analyzing patient data and simulating drug interactions, supercomputers predict an individual's response to a particular treatment, allowing clinicians to choose the most effective option.

2.3 Treatment Optimization:

Supercomputing helps optimize treatment regimens, such as chemotherapy dosages or radiation therapy plans, to maximize their therapeutic effect.

3. Disease Modeling and Simulation:

Supercomputing facilitates the simulation of complex biological systems, shedding light on disease mechanisms and potential treatment strategies:

3.1 Protein Folding and Misfolding:

Understanding protein folding, misfolding, and aggregation is crucial in diseases like Alzheimer's and Parkinson's. Supercomputers simulate these processes to identify potential drug targets.

3.2 Virus and Pathogen Modeling:

Supercomputing plays a pivotal role in modeling the behavior of viruses and pathogens, aiding in the development of vaccines and antiviral drugs, as seen during the COVID-19 pandemic.

3.3 Drug Resistance Prediction:

In infectious diseases and cancer, supercomputing predicts the development of drug resistance, guiding treatment strategies and drug development efforts.

4. Drug Repurposing:

Supercomputers analyze existing drugs' molecular properties to identify potential new uses. This approach expedites drug development, as safety data for repurposed drugs is often available.

5. Clinical Trials Optimization:

Supercomputing optimizes the design and execution of clinical trials, ensuring efficient data collection and analysis. This accelerates the development of new therapies and treatments.

Challenges and Future Directions:

While supercomputing offers transformative potential in healthcare and drug discovery, it comes with challenges:

1. Data Integration: Integrating diverse datasets, including genomics, clinical records, and drug databases, is complex but essential for personalized medicine.

2. Computational Resources: Ensuring access to high-performance computing resources is crucial for research institutions and healthcare providers.

3. Ethical and Privacy Considerations: Safeguarding patient data and ensuring ethical research practices remain paramount.

4. Validation and Clinical Translation: Translating computational findings into clinical practice requires rigorous validation and regulatory approval.

5. Collaboration: Collaborations between researchers, clinicians, pharmaceutical companies, and computational scientists are vital for success.

In conclusion, supercomputing has ushered in a new era in healthcare and drug discovery, revolutionizing how we understand, diagnose, and treat diseases. From accelerating drug development to enabling personalized medicine and simulating complex biological systems, supercomputing's impact is profound. As technology continues to advance, the promise of more effective treatments, cures for previously incurable diseases, and improved patient outcomes becomes increasingly attainable, making supercomputing an indispensable tool in the quest for better healthcare.

E. Predictions for the Supercomputing Industry: Charting the Future of Computational Power

The supercomputing industry is on the brink of a profound transformation, driven by technological advancements and the ever-expanding demands for computational power. In this chapter, we venture into the realm of predictions for the supercomputing industry, forecasting the trends and innovations that are poised to shape its future.

1. Exascale Computing and Beyond:

Prediction: The deployment of exascale supercomputers (machines capable of performing one quintillion calculations per second) will become a reality, unlocking new frontiers in scientific research, climate modeling, and engineering simulations.

Impact: Exascale computing will empower researchers to tackle previously insurmountable challenges, such as simulating complex biological systems, modeling climate change with unprecedented accuracy, and advancing materials science.

2. Quantum Advantage:

Prediction: Quantum supercomputers will continue to

advance, reaching a point where they provide a practical advantage for solving complex problems over classical supercomputers.

Impact: Quantum advantage will revolutionize fields like cryptography, optimization, and drug discovery, with applications in cybersecurity, logistics, and materials science.

3. Heterogeneous Architectures:

Prediction: Supercomputers will increasingly adopt heterogeneous architectures, combining CPUs with specialized accelerators like GPUs, FPGAs, and AI accelerators.

Impact: This fusion of hardware will enable more efficient parallel processing, accelerating a wide range of applications, from artificial intelligence and deep learning to scientific simulations.

4. AI and Supercomputing Synergy:

Prediction: Artificial intelligence and machine learning will become integral components of supercomputing workflows, enhancing data analysis, predictive modeling, and decision-making capabilities.

Impact: The synergy between AI and supercomputing will drive breakthroughs in healthcare, finance, materials science, and autonomous systems.

5. Energy Efficiency:

Prediction: Energy-efficient supercomputing will be a top priority, with innovations in cooling technologies, low-power processors, and renewable energy sources.

Impact: Sustainable supercomputing will reduce operational costs, minimize environmental impact, and enable the deployment of large-scale computing facilities.

6. Edge Supercomputing Growth:

Prediction: Edge supercomputing will proliferate, bringing high-performance computing capabilities to the network's edge, supporting real-time data processing for IoT applications.

Impact: Edge supercomputing will enable autonomous vehicles, smart cities, and industrial automation, with low-latency, mission-critical processing capabilities.

7. International Collaboration:

Prediction: Collaboration between countries and organizations will continue to grow, fostering innovation and resource sharing in the supercomputing industry.

Impact: International collaboration will drive the development of shared supercomputing facilities, joint research projects, and the exchange of expertise, benefitting global scientific progress.

8. Quantum-Safe Cryptography:

Prediction: In response to the threat posed by quantum computers to classical encryption methods, the supercomputing industry will invest in quantum-safe cryptography solutions.

Impact: Quantum-safe cryptography will protect sensitive data against quantum attacks, ensuring the security of communications and transactions.

9. Expanding Use Cases:

Prediction: Supercomputing will find applications in diverse industries, including finance, entertainment, cybersecurity, and natural resource management.

Impact: As supercomputing becomes more accessible and versatile, it will drive innovation and efficiency across a broad spectrum of sectors.

10. Ethical and Regulatory Considerations:

Prediction: Ethical concerns surrounding supercomputing, such as responsible AI use and data privacy, will lead to the development of ethical guidelines and regulations.

Impact: Ethical frameworks will guide the responsible development and deployment of supercomputing technologies, ensuring societal benefits while minimizing risks.

In conclusion, the supercomputing industry is at the cusp of an exciting era, characterized by exascale computing, quantum advantage, and the integration of AI. These predictions offer a glimpse into a future where supercomputers play an increasingly pivotal role in scientific discovery, technological innovation, and societal advancement. As the industry evolves, it must address challenges related to sustainability, ethics, and global collaboration to harness the full potential of computational power for the betterment of humanity.

Conclusion

As we draw the final curtain on this journey through these pages, we invite you to reflect on the knowledge, insights, and discoveries that have unfolded before you. Our exploration of various subjects has been a captivating voyage into the depths of understanding.

In these chapters, we have ventured through the intricacies of numerous topics and examined the key concepts and findings that define these fields. It is our hope that you have found inspiration, enlightenment, and valuable takeaways that resonate with you on your own quest for knowledge.

Remember that the pursuit of understanding is an ever-evolving journey, and this book is but a milestone along the way. The world of knowledge is vast and boundless, offering endless opportunities for exploration and growth.

As you conclude this book, we encourage you to carry forward the torch of curiosity and continue your exploration of these subjects. Seek out new perspectives, engage in meaningful discussions, and embrace the thrill of lifelong learning.

We express our sincere gratitude for joining us on this intellectual adventure. Your curiosity and dedication to expanding your horizons are the driving forces behind our shared quest for wisdom and insight.

Thank you for entrusting us with a portion of your intellectual journey. May your pursuit of knowledge lead you to new heights and inspire others to embark on their own quests for understanding.

With profound gratitude,

Nikhilesh Mishra, Author

Recap of Key Takeaways

As you conclude your comprehensive exploration of "Mastering Supercomputing: Concepts, Techniques, and Applications," it's essential to revisit and recap the key takeaways from this enriching journey. This recap serves as a compass, guiding you through the intricate landscape of supercomputing concepts, technologies, and applications you've encountered.

1. **Definition and Significance of Supercomputing:**

   - Supercomputing refers to the use of highly advanced computing systems designed for unparalleled processing power and performance.

   - The significance of supercomputing lies in its ability to tackle complex problems across various domains, from scientific research to engineering simulations and artificial intelligence.

2. **Historical Evolution of Supercomputing:**

   - Supercomputing has evolved from early mainframes and vector supercomputers to today's diverse range of architectures, including cluster systems and quantum computers.

   - Historical milestones, such as the development of Cray-1 and the emergence of parallel processing, have shaped the field.

3. **Key Concepts (Parallel Processing, Scalability):**

  - Parallel processing involves breaking down tasks into smaller subtasks that can be executed simultaneously, leading to significant performance gains.

  - Scalability is the ability of a supercomputer to maintain or improve its performance as it scales up by adding more processing units.

4. **Benefits and Challenges of Supercomputing:**

  - Benefits include accelerated scientific discoveries, improved weather predictions, advancements in drug development, and enhanced engineering simulations.

  - Challenges encompass power consumption, heat management, programming complexities, and data handling.

5. **Setting Objectives for Learning About Supercomputing:**

  - Define clear objectives for your supercomputing journey, whether it's mastering parallel programming, delving into quantum computing, or advancing a specific domain.

6. **Parallel Computing Fundamentals:**

  - Parallel processing is crucial for supercomputing, enabling efficient task execution and data processing.

  - Types of parallelism, including data and task

parallelism, offer diverse approaches to harnessing parallel computing power.

7. **Parallel Architectures (SIMD, MIMD):**

   - SIMD (Single Instruction, Multiple Data) and MIMD (Multiple Instruction, Multiple Data) architectures cater to different parallel processing requirements.

   - Understanding these architectures is essential for choosing the right hardware for specific applications.

8. **Message Passing and Shared Memory Models:**

   - Message passing involves communication between separate processors, typical in distributed memory systems.

   - Shared memory models allow multiple processors to access a common memory pool, common in multi-core architectures.

9. **Scalability and Performance Metrics:**

   - Scalability metrics assess a supercomputer's ability to handle increasing workloads efficiently.

   - Performance metrics, like FLOPS (Floating-Point Operations Per Second) and MPI (Message Passing Interface) benchmarks, quantify computational efficiency.

This recap serves as a foundational summary of the key insights you've gained throughout your journey. It's a testament to your dedication to mastering supercomputing, a field that continues to redefine the boundaries of what's computationally possible. As you apply these takeaways to your future endeavors in supercomputing, remember that your pursuit of knowledge and innovation is boundless. Your journey in this ever-evolving field has just begun, and the possibilities are limitless.

The Future of Supercomputing

As we stand at the intersection of technological innovation and computational prowess, the future of supercomputing promises to be an exhilarating journey into uncharted territory. "Mastering Supercomputing: Concepts, Techniques, and Applications" has equipped you with the knowledge to appreciate not only where supercomputing stands today but also the exciting possibilities that lie ahead.

1. **Exascale Computing and Beyond:**

The foremost frontier in supercomputing is achieving exascale computing, wherein a supercomputer can perform a quintillion (10^{18}) calculations per second. This unprecedented level of computational power opens doors to solving problems that were previously inconceivable due to their sheer complexity. Applications range from simulating intricate biological processes to accurately modeling climate change.

Beyond exascale, the path leads to zettascale and yottascale computing, where computing power continues to grow exponentially. These milestones will enable the simulation of even more complex systems, such as entire ecosystems or detailed models of the human brain.

2. **Quantum Supercomputing and Quantum Advantage:**

Quantum supercomputing represents a paradigm shift in computing. Quantum computers leverage the principles of quantum mechanics to perform calculations that would take classical supercomputers eons to complete. They excel in solving optimization problems, cryptography, and simulating quantum systems, which are inherently quantum in nature.

Achieving "quantum advantage" refers to the point at which quantum computers outperform classical supercomputers for specific tasks. While quantum computing is still in its infancy, it holds enormous potential for revolutionizing fields like materials science, drug discovery, and cryptography.

3. **Edge Supercomputing and IoT:**

The proliferation of the Internet of Things (IoT) and the need for real-time data analysis are driving the development of edge supercomputing. These compact yet powerful devices bring supercomputing capabilities to the edge of networks, allowing rapid data processing at the source. Edge supercomputers will be instrumental in applications like autonomous vehicles, smart cities, and industrial automation.

4. **Supercomputing for Healthcare and Drug Discovery:**

The healthcare industry is poised to benefit significantly from supercomputing. Personalized medicine, which tailors treatments to an individual's genetic makeup, relies heavily on computational simulations. Supercomputers can analyze vast genomic datasets, predict disease risk, and simulate drug interactions, accelerating drug discovery and advancing patient care.

5. **Sustainability and Green Supercomputing:**

As the demand for computational power grows, so does the energy consumption of supercomputers. Green supercomputing focuses on developing energy-efficient architectures and cooling solutions to mitigate the environmental impact. Future supercomputers will need to strike a balance between performance and sustainability, using renewable energy sources and novel cooling techniques.

6. **International Collaboration in Supercomputing:**

Supercomputing is a global endeavor, and international collaboration is essential. Initiatives like the European Union's EuroHPC and international partnerships for research and development promote knowledge sharing and resource pooling. Collaborative efforts pave the way for solving global challenges through collective computational power.

7. **Interdisciplinary Applications:**

The future of supercomputing is inherently interdisciplinary. As computational methods become more accessible and versatile, they will permeate fields beyond traditional scientific research. Industries like finance, entertainment, and urban planning will harness supercomputing for data analysis, modeling, and optimization.

In conclusion, the future of supercomputing is a tapestry of innovation, collaboration, and limitless possibilities. As you continue your journey in this field, remember that you are a part of a dynamic community driving technological advancement. The skills and insights you've gained from "Mastering Supercomputing" position you to be a pioneer in shaping this exciting future, where computational power knows no bounds. Embrace the challenges, explore the frontiers, and push the limits of what supercomputing can achieve. The future is yours to define.

Glossary of Terms

Navigating the world of supercomputing can be akin to traversing a labyrinth of technical jargon and acronyms. To aid your mastery of this domain, here's an in-depth glossary of supercomputing terms that will unravel the intricacies of this fascinating field.

1. Supercomputing:

- Supercomputing refers to the use of high-performance computing systems that offer exceptional processing power and speed. Supercomputers are employed for computationally intensive tasks such as scientific simulations, data analysis, and complex modeling.

2. Exascale Computing:

- Exascale computing is the next frontier in high-performance computing, signifying the ability to perform a quintillion (10^{18}) calculations per second. Achieving exascale computing requires groundbreaking advances in hardware and software.

3. Parallel Processing:

- Parallel processing is a computing technique where multiple processors work simultaneously on different parts of a task, enhancing computational speed and efficiency. It is fundamental to supercomputing.

4. Scalability:

•   Scalability is the capability of a system, application, or hardware to handle increasing workloads without compromising performance. It is a critical factor in supercomputer design.

5. SIMD (Single Instruction, Multiple Data):

•   SIMD is a type of parallel architecture where a single instruction is executed on multiple data elements simultaneously. It is commonly used in multimedia and graphics processing.

6. MIMD (Multiple Instruction, Multiple Data):

•   MIMD is another parallel architecture where multiple instructions can be executed on multiple data elements simultaneously. It is more versatile and is employed in various supercomputer designs.

7. Message Passing:

•   Message passing is a communication model in supercomputing where separate processors exchange data by passing messages. This model is used in distributed memory systems.

8. Shared Memory Model:

- In the shared memory model, multiple processors can access a common memory pool. It is prevalent in multi-core and symmetric multiprocessing (SMP) architectures.

9. High-Performance Interconnects:

- High-performance interconnects are specialized networking technologies that enable high-speed data transfer between processors and memory units in a supercomputer.

10. High-Performance Storage Systems: - These are advanced storage solutions designed to meet the high bandwidth and low latency requirements of supercomputers. They include parallel file systems and solid-state drives.

11. HPC (High-Performance Computing) Libraries: - HPC libraries are software components that provide optimized routines and functions for numerical computations, making it easier to develop high-performance applications.

12. FLOPS (Floating-Point Operations Per Second): - FLOPS is a metric used to measure the computational performance of supercomputers. It quantifies the number of floating-point operations a computer can perform in one second.

13. MPI (Message Passing Interface): - MPI is a standardized communication protocol used in high-performance computing for message passing between processes or nodes in a cluster.

14. CUDA (Compute Unified Device Architecture): - CUDA is a parallel computing platform and application programming interface (API) developed by NVIDIA. It is used for GPU (Graphics Processing Unit) programming and acceleration.

15. Quantum Supercomputers: - Quantum supercomputers leverage the principles of quantum mechanics to perform calculations that are beyond the capabilities of classical supercomputers. They use quantum bits or qubits for processing.

16. Edge Supercomputing: - Edge supercomputing refers to the deployment of supercomputing capabilities at the network edge, enabling real-time data processing and analysis for IoT and other applications.

17. Green Supercomputing: - Green supercomputing focuses on designing energy-efficient supercomputers to reduce power consumption and environmental impact.

18. Supercomputing Cluster: - A supercomputing cluster is a group of interconnected computers that work together to solve complex problems, sharing computational tasks.

19. Quantum Advantage: - Quantum advantage is achieved when a quantum computer outperforms classical supercomputers for specific tasks, marking a significant milestone in quantum computing.

20. Supercomputing Center: - A supercomputing center is a facility equipped with high-performance computing resources, including supercomputers, used for research, simulations, and data analysis.

This glossary serves as a valuable reference as you continue your journey in mastering supercomputing. Understanding these terms will empower you to navigate the complexities of this field with confidence and expertise.

Resources and References

As you reach the final pages of this book by Nikhilesh Mishra, consider it not an ending but a stepping stone. The pursuit of knowledge is an unending journey, and the world of information is boundless.

Discover a World Beyond These Pages

We extend a warm invitation to explore a realm of boundless learning and discovery through our dedicated online platform: **www.nikhileshmishra.com**. Here, you will unearth a carefully curated trove of resources and references to empower your quest for wisdom.

Unleash the Potential of Your Mind

- **Diital Libraries:** Immerse yourself in vast digital libraries, granting access to books, research papers, and academic treasures.

- **Interactive Courses:** Engage with interactive courses and lectures from world-renowned institutions, nurturing your thirst for knowledge.

- **Enlightening Talks:** Be captivated by enlightening talks delivered by visionaries and experts from diverse fields.

- **Community Connections:** Connect with a global community of like-minded seekers, engage in meaningful discussions, and share your knowledge journey.

Your Journey Has Just Begun

Your journey as a seeker of knowledge need not end here. Our website awaits your exploration, offering a gateway to an infinite universe of insights and references tailored to ignite your intellectual curiosity.

Acknowledgments

As I stand at this pivotal juncture, reflecting upon the completion of this monumental work, I am overwhelmed with profound gratitude for the exceptional individuals who have been instrumental in shaping this remarkable journey.

In Loving Memory

To my father, **Late Shri Krishna Gopal Mishra,** whose legacy of wisdom and strength continues to illuminate my path, even in his physical absence, I offer my deepest respect and heartfelt appreciation.

The Pillars of Support

My mother, **Mrs. Vijay Kanti Mishra,** embodies unwavering resilience and grace. Your steadfast support and unwavering faith in my pursuits have been the bedrock of my journey.

To my beloved wife, **Mrs. Anshika Mishra,** your unshakable belief in my abilities has been an eternal wellspring of motivation. Your constant encouragement has propelled me to reach new heights.

My daughter, **Miss Aarvi Mishra,** infuses my life with boundless joy and unbridled inspiration. Your insatiable curiosity serves as a constant reminder of the limitless power of exploration and discovery.

Brothers in Arms

To my younger brothers, **Mr. Ashutosh Mishra** and **Mr. Devashish Mishra,** who have steadfastly stood by my side, offering unwavering support and shared experiences that underscore the strength of familial bonds.

A Journey Shared

This book is a testament to the countless hours of dedication and effort that have gone into its creation. I am immensely grateful for the privilege of sharing my knowledge and insights with a global audience.

Readers, My Companions

To all the readers who embark on this intellectual journey alongside me, your curiosity and unquenchable thirst for knowledge inspire me to continually push the boundaries of understanding in the realm of cloud computing.

With profound appreciation and sincere gratitude,

Nikhilesh Mishra

September 08, 2023

About the Author

Nikhilesh Mishra is an extraordinary visionary, propelled by an insatiable curiosity and an unyielding passion for innovation. With a relentless commitment to exploring the boundaries of knowledge and technology, Nikhilesh has embarked on an exceptional journey to unravel the intricate complexities of our world.

Hailing from the vibrant and diverse landscape of India, Nikhilesh's pursuit of knowledge has driven him to plunge deep into the world of discovery and understanding from a remarkably young age. His unwavering determination and quest for innovation have not only cemented his position as a thought leader but have also earned him global recognition in the ever-evolving realm of technology and human understanding.

Over the years, Nikhilesh has not only mastered the art of translating complex concepts into accessible insights but has also crafted a unique talent for inspiring others to explore the limitless possibilities of human potential.

Nikhilesh's journey transcends the mere boundaries of expertise; it is a transformative odyssey that challenges conventional wisdom and redefines the essence of exploration. His commitment to pushing the boundaries and reimagining the norm serves as a luminous beacon of inspiration to all those who aspire to make a profound impact in the world of knowledge.

Mastering Supercomputing

As you navigate the intricate corridors of human understanding and innovation, you will not only gain insight into Nikhilesh's expertise but also experience his unwavering dedication to empowering readers like you. Prepare to be enthralled as he seamlessly melds intricate insights with real-world applications, igniting the flames of curiosity and innovation within each reader.

Nikhilesh Mishra's work extends beyond the realm of authorship; it is a reflection of his steadfast commitment to shaping the future of knowledge and exploration. It is an embodiment of his boundless dedication to disseminating wisdom for the betterment of individuals worldwide.

Prepare to be inspired, enlightened, and empowered as you embark on this transformative journey alongside Nikhilesh Mishra. Your understanding of the world will be forever enriched, and your passion for exploration and innovation will reach new heights under his expert guidance.

Sincerely, **A Fellow Explorer**

Notes

Notes

Notes

Notes

Notes

Notes

Notes

Notes